The
Floral Home

The
Floral Home

LESLIE GEDDES-BROWN

CROWN PUBLISHERS, INC., NEW YORK

To Daphne Stevenson, my mother-in-law,
who taught me to appreciate flowers

Edited and designed by Mitchell Beazley Publishers
part of Reed International Books Ltd
Michelin House, 81 Fulham Road, London SW3 6RB

Design Director **Jacqui Small**
Executive Editor **Judith More**
Editor **Mary Davies**
Assistant Art Editor **Trinity Fry**
Editorial Assistants **Jaspal Bhangra, Catherine Smith**
Production **Sarah Schuman**

Published by Crown Publishers, Inc., 201 East 50th Street, New York,
New York 10022. Member of the Crown Publishing Group.
Published in Great Britain by Mitchell Beazley Publishers in 1992.
CROWN is a registered trademark of Crown Publishers, Inc.

Manufactured in Hong Kong.

Library of Congress Cataloging-in-Publication Data
Geddes-Brown, Leslie.
    The floral home: from floral wallpapers and fabrics to arranging
fresh and dried flowers, the complete guide to decorating with
flowers / Leslie Geddes-Brown.
        p.   cm.
    1. Interior decoration - - Themes, motives. 2. Decoration and
ornament - - Plant forms. 3. Flowers in art. I. Title.
NK2113.G43   1992
747 - - dc20   91-39122 CIP

ISBN 0-517-58833-1

10 9 8 7 6 5 4 3 2 1

First American Edition
The publishers have made every effort to ensure that all instructions given in this book are accurate
and safe, but they cannot accept liability for any resulting injury, damage or loss to either person
or property whether direct or consequential and howsoever arising. The author and publishers
will be grateful for any information which will assist them in keeping future editions up to date.

Typeset in Stempel Garamond, Roman 12/15 pt and Italic 10/12 pt
by Litho Link Ltd, Welshpool, Powys, Wales
Produced by Mandarin Offset Printed in Hong Kong

Contents

Introduction

Does it surprise you that people have decorated houses with flowers for over 4,500 years? Animals are an even older motif, it is true, but a beautifully detailed wallpainting from Maidum in Egypt that shows geese grazing on a carpet of grasses and tiny red flowers dates from 2550 BC and, because it is so fine, was clearly not the first on such a theme.

It is extraordinary how floral art crops up in every century and every civilization. Indeed, if a tribe or nation does not respect and re-create the beauties of nature, it has little claim to be called civilized. Floral art links us all. The ancient Egyptians revered the iris, which symbolized elegance (two were carved on their temple at Karnak around 1500 BC). Three thousand years later, each time Queen Isabella of Castile opened her Book of Hours she saw a portrait of *Iris germanica*, which to her was a symbol both of royalty and the Virgin Mary. Another of the Madonna's flowers was the lily and yet the crown imperial, so popular among Renaissance painters, also turns up, inlaid in semi-precious stones, on the tombs of Mumtaz Mahal and Shah Jahan in the Taj Mahal in northern India, while the wild lily is found, 220 years later still, on an embroidery by the Pre-Raphaelite New York designer Candace Wheeler.

It is a mistake to identify floral art and decoration only with the chintzy, the countrified and the cosy – though all these styles have tremendous charm. Flowers can be architectural (the Greeks used palm and acanthus leaves for their capitals), political (roses and thistles were secret Jacobite signs) and perhaps even sinister (the bloodthirsty Aztecs cultivated dahlias and zinnias). Flowers in decor are just as rich in variety. For example, the Tuscan-red dining room illustrated on page 84 is both formal and stately whereas a derelict villa I discovered actually in Tuscany, where flowers and birds were painted onto the ceiling of each state room, was nothing short of palatial. By contrast, the Cecil bedroom at Winterthur in Delaware in the north-eastern United States amalgamates tree of life bedhangings and curtains or drapes with Scandinavian green panelling to create a strong, spartan interior whereas at Wightwick Manor in England the all-over floral patterns of William Morris and his peers cover every wall, floor, tile and painting to sensuous effect.

The Floral Home draws all these various strands together to show how decoration today has been influenced by styles far distant in geography and time. Its aim is to inspire you to explore floral design in depth. The book begins with an historical survey of the ingredients now available to the floral decorator: the carpets from France, Persia and the plains of Middle America; the painted floors and inlaid tables of northern Europe and America; porcelain from China and pottery from England.

In the second part of the book, I have tried to demonstrate how many forms floral design can take. Just as flowers themselves grow from bud to bloom, so the patterns may be spriggy or blowsy, monochrome or bright, ancient or modern. Some have roots in the East, others in the West.

The heart of the book, however, is concerned with specific colours and specific rooms. Flowers unfold in every colour of the spectrum and legends have grown up around many of them. Taking individual rooms, we show how each tone and shade can be used both separately and together and how flower arrangements can complement each colour.

The book illustrates how some of the best decorators around today use the flowers and floral art on offer – and what a choice they have. Unlike our ancestors, we can draw on the world for our designs, collecting and mixing the flowers and floral art of nations as never before. As I write, I have beside me a copy of a Pompeiian fresco of Flora made into a lampshade, a pair of chairs embroidered with tulips by my great-aunt and, in a corner, a screen showing geese wandering on grasses just like that 4,500-year-old Egyptian painting – but it is from Japan. That Japanese artist had probably never seen the older version but, 4,400 years and almost half a world apart, two painters had something in common. If we, too, love and welcome flowers into our homes, then we join that great daisy chain over 40 centuries old.

Rosy-patterned chintz at the window and on the quilt present the pink and white theme but note floral variations on the lacy window drape, the mound of pillows on the bed, the posy of bright flowers on the bedside table or nightstand and the pretty porcelain plate above the bed.

Picking Floral
Ingredients

The Lore of Flowers   NEIL EWART

ROSES FOR AN EMPRESS   Josephine Bonaparte & Pierre-Joseph Redouté

RECREATING THE PERIOD GARDEN

Textiles

Until people felt moderately secure from the threats of banditry and war, they were not greatly concerned about decor. For example, interiors as we now know them arrived in Britain only in the 16th century with knotted, woven or painted carpets underfoot and, on the walls, rich tapestries or woven wools and silks. Printed textiles were virtually unknown. But even a turbulent society needed something to keep out the cold and from the late 15th century onward, for the rich and powerful, tapestries were the solution. Henry VIII was known to have at least 2,000, most of which came from the Low Countries. Verdures were among the most popular designs – all-over patterns of textured leaves and flowers, alive with birds and animals. Gradually, as the fashion for tapestries spread, factories started up in Paris, Munich, London and Rome but the battle was won by the French after Louis XIV state-aided the weavers at Gobelins, Beauvais and Aubusson. The extent of his success is reflected in the fact that these three names have come to symbolize 18th-century tapestry work – and carpets.

The French had the design edge too, aided by Louis' interest in hiring fine artists as designers. People grew tired of the heavy Baroque designs of the Dutch with their brawny scenes of hunts and gods and, by the end of the 17th century, began to favour the delicate flower traceries, Rococo arabesques and grotesqueries of French artists such as Charles Lebrun, Claude Audran III and the flower painter Jean-Baptiste Monnoyer. Then Louis XIV

made the mistake of outlawing the Protestant Huguenots in the Revocation of the Edict of Nantes in 1685 and those who fled to Britain encouraged the textile arts there. Silk weaving began in the Spitalfields district and tapestry in Soho, both in London, and carpet weaving in Exeter, in Devon, all under French influence.

However, by the late 18th century the demand for tapestry was in sharp decline. This was partly because the fashionable Neoclassical decorators did not want to detract from their fine decor and plasterwork, but also because of the arrival in the West of printed cottons from India and Persia and Europe's swift adoption of their designs and techniques. Eastern chintzes had been well known in the 17th century – around 1640 the English diarist Samuel Pepys was commenting on his wife's bedroom fabric. But Europe had also quickly developed its own printed cottons, creating fine landscapes and flowers with copperplate engravings. These are known by the generic term *toiles de Jouy*, after the Oberkampf factory near Versailles, but similar pieces were being made in England at the same time, if not earlier. In 1758 the American author, inventor, scientist and diplomat Benjamin Franklin, visiting London, bought 56 yards (51 metres) "of cotton printed curiously from copper plate" to send home to his wife for bedhangings and curtains or drapes. Themes included landscapes, hunting scenes, florals and Chinoiserie. By the early 19th century, roller-printed fabrics were available throughout Europe, looking remarkably like those on offer

Whole bouquets of tapestry flowers adorn these chairs (above) made in the style of Louis XV for the Palais de Compiègne, France. The designs were worked specially but show how a printed large-repeat fabric can decorate an upholstered chair. The faded tones of an old handmade quilt and a bone-white wicker sofa (opposite) encourage banks of multicoloured floral cushions or pillows.

Flowery Moorcroft pottery inspired the hanging in a 17th-century oak-panelled dining room (above) whereas most of the textiles in the living room (right) derive from 18th-century French motifs.

today. Designs included rose garlands interspersed with pillars, sprays of violets on monochrome floral backgrounds and striped chintzes with bouquets of flowers intermixed.

The fashion for needlework followed roughly the same pattern as that for tapestry. When fabric printing was in its infancy, needlework of all kinds flourished. A series of interiors painted by the 17th-century Flemish artist Jan van der Straet, who worked mostly in Italy, gives some indication of the popularity of the craft in Europe. One shows a large group of women embroidering at home and another demonstrates that silk worms were cultivated domestically for the work.

As in all textile design, the influences were confused. Blackwork was one of the early popular forms of embroidery. Inspired by the Moors in Spain, it consisted of tapestry-like patterns of complex florals stitched in black silk on a white ground. In Britain, there was a great flowering of interest in embroidery in the second half of the 16th century because the Reformation had released skilled workers from ecclesiastical employment. Cutlery holders, book covers and markers and linen pouches were all made in floral needlework.

Needlework was also used to copy the scarce Oriental rugs of the period, and not only in Europe. In the 17th century, a remarkable effort by the Ursuline nuns in Quebec resulted in European floral patterns being created in Amerindian fashion, with feather quills. Nearly 4,000 years before, embroidery was already in full flower in China, where it remains little changed today. In 1861, the Regent Empress Tsu Hsi ordered her

embroiderers to work beside the Summer Palace in Peking. Patterns were copied from flowers set by the workers. However, in Europe by the late 18th century embroiderers were turning to small framed pieces, a prelude to the 19th-century fashion for Berlin woolwork devotional scenes and landscapes.

The Chinese probably also invented quilting, which was originally used to deflect spears and arrows. Almost certainly the Crusaders brought it to Europe after they learned its military uses from the Arabs. However, by the 16th century, quilting was being used for bedcovers and warm clothes. Worked in running stitch, patterns were traditional in certain areas.

Quilts were made all over Europe and in North America, and superstitions grew up around them. For example, marriage quilts

Palmer of Otsego County, New York. Between circles of white fabric, stuffed and sewn in patterns of grapes and fruit baskets so that they appear blind printed, are appliquéd wreaths of old-fashioned pink roses, buds and green leaves. Later quilts were made in simple flowered chintz and stitched over and around the patterns. A recent fashion has revived the technique.

Unlike quilting, patchwork is an art which sprang solely from deprivation and poverty (not necessarily the same thing, as American colonists found in the 18th century when printed cotton imports were forbidden to them by the Hanoverians). Patchwork as a technique (using leather) goes back at least 3,000 years, and fabric patchwork was used as long ago as the 6th century AD. However, the patterns now associated with

Linen, cotton and lace mix to make a bright summery room (right) which combines traditional elements in an uncluttered modern style. Note the window curtains or drapes, where floral lace backed by plain cotton creates an interesting new texture. Floral textiles in traditional English decor are sometimes a brave marriage of styles and periods: (opposite, top left) Jacobean-style bedhangings, a 19th-century patchwork quilt and a kelim-covered seat all demand attention, whereas (opposite, top right) in a more restrained scheme, the tiny all-over pattern on an Oriental rug complements a modern print fabric which is based on crewelwork flower and foliage motifs. Needlework enables you to bring intricate floral detail to a traditional living room (opposite, middle left); see, for example, the exquisite ribboned garlands which decorate the curtains or drapes.

You can mix different textures and styles in a floral textile scheme provided that the colours are well chosen (opposite, middle right); here a dusty rose-red from the Oriental carpet is echoed on a European rug and in the self-patterned damask cushions or pillows on the kelim-covered Chesterfield sofa. But sometimes even more effectively, as in an austere gothic setting (opposite, bottom left), a single outstanding textile such as these 17th-century crewelwork tree of life hanging panels can be left simply to speak for itself, alongside a modern elm coffer by Richard Latrobe Bateman and a pair of Arts and Crafts candlesticks. In contrast (opposite, bottom right), a striped, self-patterned floral damask on the walls and a beautiful 18th-century Aubusson carpet combine in sombre splendour to demonstrate the formality of stylized period floral patterns.

could be embellished with roses and hearts but brides-to-be were not allowed to work them. There are masterpiece quilts that tested sewers' skills to the utmost and medallion quilts with a central embroidered or appliquéd picture. Patterns were often worked on white fabrics or sewn in contrasting strips.

Although they were made largely by the pioneers and those too poor to buy their own, quilts were also created for the upper classes. For skill and luxury there are few examples which surpass a quilt of yellow silk sewn in 1680, now on display in London's Victoria and Albert Museum. It has geometrical borders but the middle, stitched in rope pattern, is of free-form flowering plants, including lilies and oak leaves. Yet it is no more elegant than a treasure in Washington's Smithsonian Museum: a mid 19th-century padded and appliquéd quilt made by Mary and Deborah

patchwork generally came into their own when printed cottons began to arrive from the East. Supply fell so short of the demand that cut-offs were put together for bedcovers and the like.

In the United States, patchwork seemed to grow in celebration of the Revolution – and ending of the import controls. It is really only here that the craft became an art form as patterns like Grandmother's Flower Garden and French Bouquet evolved. Today, antique American quilts fetch thousands of dollars, especially if they have a provenance or are signed by the maker, and the fabric mixes are a valuable source for historical research.

The United States also improved on the old European craft of making rugs from unwanted scraps, using anything from knitted woollens to velvet, worsted and serge. European patterns were essentially random or geometric, but in the United States by 1824

*Floral tapestry chairs do not need to match to look good.
The whole series of different styles and patterns on this
collection of French 18th- and 19th-century furniture
is mutually complementary, but it is an approach
which demands a spacious interior. Note how cleverly
the other furniture and decorative objects have been
chosen. Rich in interest and textural detail, they have
been kept deliberately low in conflicting colours.
The self-patterned damask on the sofa, the muted rose-
decked carpet, the opulent but almost monochromatic
ornaments and simple shuttered windows all
contribute to this controlled effect.*

great bouquets of flowers or patterns of leaves, birds, grapes and daisies were being used, as in the earliest dated yarn-sewn rug yet discovered. Another, of rags and probably not much later in date, found in Massachusetts, has a formal pattern of urns overflowing with exotic flowers and leaves, all on a black background with a stylized leaf border.

With so many inspirational pieces around, it is not surprising that the craft of rugmaking with rags or scraps of wool has been revived. The methods are simple but arduous. The cloth can be cut into short strips and pushed through a hessian or burlap backing so that both ends poke upward; alternatively longer pieces can be threaded in and out of the backing several times to make a smoother, humped surface. If they are closely worked on strong hessian or burlap, these rugs will cope with the heaviest wear and last for years.

The earliest known carpets date back thousands of years – and, with them, floral motifs that are still extant today. For example, only 50 years ago a pile carpet was discovered in Scythia in Central Asia that dates back to the 3rd century BC, while at Nineveh, the heart of the Assyrian Empire, a stonemason in the 7th century BC is known to have worked a pavement that copied a long-vanished carpet. And Oriental carpets, which traditionally mix flowers and animals with geometrical motifs, were laid on floors and furniture in ancient Greece and Rome, the first

examples of that intermingling of Eastern and Western influences so characteristic of textile history.

However, the people of the Dark Ages were not interested in carpets and they disappeared in the West for centuries only to re-emerge through East-West contact following Arab conquests around the Mediterranean and the Crusades. For example, we know that in 1255 Eleanor of Castile decked her rooms in London with rugs because the English joked about them.

Rich Eastern carpets appear in scores of the paintings of the Renaissance, hanging from Florentine windows, under the feet of enthroned virgins, in Hans Holbein's portrait *The French Ambassadors* and Hans Eworth's of Henry VIII of England. Indeed, early carpet patterns are known as Holbeins, Memlings and Lottos after examples found in those painters' work.

English needlework designs of flowering plants made the journey back to the Orient, where they found favour with the Mughal rulers of India. Shah Jahan, who ruled between 1628 and 1658, encouraged European botanical designs, whereas his predecessor, Shah Abbas, oversaw the introduction of the famous vase patterns. In the later 18th century architect-decorators preferred the European designs of Aubusson, Savonnerie and Axminster, which could be worked to imitate the plaster ceilings of the day. But once they reached Europe, Oriental carpets never really went out of fashion again.

Three needlepoint carpets from Vigo based on original designs: (below, middle) an adaptation of a late 18th-century design and (below, left and right) two derived from 19th-century work.

Complementary textiles can bond a scheme to memorable effect (opposite), as in the soft colours of a tulip-strewn rug from Colefax and Fowler and a chintz from the same company.

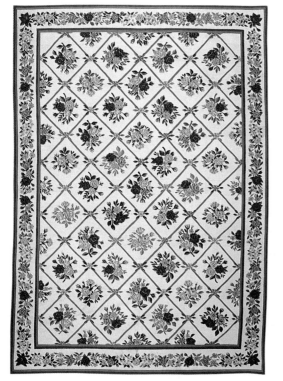

Surfaces

Simple painted flower and water symbols sing out against the gray-washed walls in this bathroom at painter Vanessa Bell's country home at Charleston, Sussex, England (right). The room was decorated in the early 20th century by fellow members of the Bloomsbury Group, a London-based literary and artistic set who often used the house as a retreat.

The light fantastic of Rococo style decorates the walls of a charming bedroom in a French chateau (opposite). An exquisite tracery of stylized flowers hangs about the garlands and swags of identifiable blooms which surround vignettes of surprisingly savage encounters in the animal kingdom. The bedcover is embroidered with equal delicacy.

*E*arly wallpaper was always the poor relation of silk damask, tapestry or embossed leather so few pieces survive. But, almost from the beginning, floral patterns seem to have been the most common. Through the centuries, paper has been made to imitate damask, *toile de Jouy*, lace, gilded borders and murals – and always with the aid of flowers. For example, some of the very earliest designs pretended to be blackwork embroideries, while the latest, from firms like Laura Ashley, include pastiches of floral patchwork quilts or authentic 18th-century sprigs.

One of the earliest surviving real wallpapers yet discovered was found in Britain, in the Master's Lodge of Christ's College, Cambridge, and it proves that in 1509 images of plants were certainly being papered onto walls. Probably made by Hugo Goes, from Beverley, in Yorkshire, it copied a "split pomegranate" pattern frequently found on silk damask. A later Tudor paper of c. 1560 from Besford Court, Worcestershire, is more directly floral, being coarsely printed with stylized vases of flowers.

By the 18th century, wallpaper-making was in full swing and technically brilliant, although still considered second-best. French designer J-B Reveillon of Paris was creating complex, full-colour panels of Arcadian landscapes after the contemporary painter Jean Honoré Fragonard, surrounded by flowered cartouches, or, for the American market, eagles holding garlands of flowers. In England, on the other hand, wallpapers were already beginning to copy Indian chintz and use flock for extra richness. Some of the simpler designs of that period vary little from those most popular today, while the 18th-century extravagances of the French factory of Zuber are once more hugely popular.

In the second half of the 19th century, wallpaper began to gain a better reputation as great designers and architects treated it seriously. In Britain, Augustus W.N. Pugin created a whole series for the Houses of Parliament, and in 1880 William Morris designed a stylized floral pattern for the throne room at St James's Palace, in London. Vines, bamboo, daisies, pinks, columbine, even whole orchards, were all immortalized on paper.

There is currently a huge international interest in old papers, inspired by the desire to use authentic materials in house redecoration. Original scraps and collections that appear on the market are quickly bought up. Firms such as Zoffany and the Design Archive in Britain, Zuber in France and Brunschwig in the United States provenance and date surviving pieces, and old wood blocks are brought out to re-create the designs of the past. As country houses are redecorated, reproduction papers, like reproduction fabrics, are being hung so it is easy to see how our forebears used their floral borders and dadoes, the formal ceiling papers and wallpapers. If accuracy is your aim, copy them.

One of the earliest crazes in wallpaper design took place in the 16th century when the discovery of the Emperor Nero's palace in Rome led to a passion for walls decorated with landscapes,

Stencilled floral motifs create a naively striped wall in a typical 19th-century American bedroom reconstructed at the American Museum in Bath, England (left), in contrast with the elegant simplicity of the hand-painted flower friezes and vases set upon pedestals above a dado in a Swedish country house which dates from the same period (above).

grotesques and garlands. Of course, Nero's walls were painted – there is no evidence of wallpaper before the 11th century, and then only of religious prints used like posters – but in the 16th century those who could not afford murals made do with paper.

Today wallpaper is so commonplace that few people consider murals (and perhaps even fewer live anywhere long enough to make the undertaking worthwhile). Nonetheless, there has been a remarkable revival in wallpainting led, perhaps, by English artists such as Rex Whistler working in World War II. Today's artists take inspiration from his landscapes as well as from antiquity, using garlands and bouquets of flowers, figures in pastoral settings and the vines and trellises of the interiors of Pompeii. Indeed, the discovery of the Roman town, south of Naples, buried by lava from Mount Vesuvius in 79AD, has remained a constant inspiration to mural painters since excavations began in 1784. Today Carlos Marchiori, working in the United States, and Ricardo Cinalli, in Great Britain, use the same classical themes, and the J. Paul Getty Museum in Malibu, California, has a room swagged with Pompeiian flowers and garlands painted by the American muralist Garth Benton.

Trompe l'oeil is also very fashionable. There are *faux* fireplaces filled with *faux* floral porcelain and surmounted by *faux* flowers on *faux* shelves. Italian artist Lucretia Moroni has even painted an entire floor with a *faux* floral Oriental carpet in a Manhattan

Sunflowers are the only identifiable flowers on this 19th-century painted chest of drawers. A collection of boxes, potpourri and wonderfully colour-matched roses extends the floral theme.

This simple old pine chest was decorated by Mary Wondrausch, a potter much influenced by folk art. In summertime a vase of sweet peas and alchemilla heightens the colours she has chosen.

townhouse. Of course, painted carpets and dummy boards of vases of Chinese porcelain were first undertaken because they were cheaper than the real thing. Or, in the United States and Australia, the only possibility. The pioneers were extremely clever in their use of such techniques. Walls, floors and canvases laid on floors were frequently stencilled with all-over repeating patterns or borders to imitate wallpaper, tapestry or floral swags and printed blooms or bouquets were stuck onto all manner of objects. Decoupage, or the art of decorating surfaces with illustrations cut from card or paper, produced objects of great charm and American hatboxes can still be seen in museum collections, their sides glued with roses, landscapes and political slogans and then varnished.

Stencilling, along with other paint techniques, has had a recent vogue and numerous books have been written about its history and method. However, it is at risk from over-popularity and something of its dash and vigour are in danger of being lost. To see it at its best, it is advisable to go back to pioneering days. Museums are also a good source of early stencilling techniques.

Floorspreads, of course, were not the invention of the colonies. They turned up in the early 18th century throughout Europe (generally in servants' quarters or poorer houses) to imitate carpets and mosaics. This is another skill which has been revived quite recently. Some patterns copied the floral marquetry

fashionable in Europe during the mid-17th century. Symmetrical and formal, they were also influenced by parterre garden designs or, of course, by tapestries and carpets.

Painting objects to look grander than they were was not confined to floors. Furniture was also grained with floral marquetry patterns. Louis XVI secretaires were inlaid with exotic woods to create patterns of flowers, bowls of fruit, even whole interiors, but this required immense skill on the part of the cabinet maker. Painting the surfaces was not only a great deal easier, it was also more effective. Scagliola designs of coloured *faux* marble also copied the intricate florals of *pietra dura*.

Painted furniture also crops up in the vernacular tradition throughout Europe. Cheerful flowers were often painted on brightly varnished or stained wooden backgrounds to disguise the faults of the wood beneath. And there were similar patterns – with roses almost invariably cropping up somewhere – on the cupboards, beds and kitchen implements of the barges which crossed and re-crossed Europe along the main river arteries.

Such traditions quickly found their way to the New World, not only on floors, walls and furniture but also on ceramics and tole ware. Other, more sophisticated designs from Scandinavia, combining marbling and graining with over-painted stencilled or free-hand bouquets or garlands of flowers, also made the journey across the Atlantic.

Decorative Objects

*Framed like watercolours in matching mounts,
botanical prints can be symmetrically displayed in
formal groups to great effect in a style typical of the
English country house.*

We know books of botanical drawings were in use before the birth of Christ because Pliny the Elder mentions Roman artists who compiled illustrated herbals. Of course, illustrations in the earliest herbals were drawn and painted but by the 14th century AD German printers were making detailed woodcuts which were then hand-coloured. Such books concentrated on itemizing what plants would cure which ailments but in the 16th century, as the voyages of discovery got gradually underway, botanists and artists began to record the plants of newly discovered continents.

The discovery of Australasia led to a wonderful series of volumes, *Banks's Florilegium*, which was only printed in its complete form in the 1970s, although the original line engravings were made between 1775 and 1780. Drawn and engraved by several artists, they are the Audubons of the plant world but it was not until the arrival of Pierre Joseph Redouté, the most well-known of all botanical artists, that full-colour prints were made. In 1796, he claimed to have invented the colour-stipple engraving technique which produced incredibly detailed and sensitive portraits of the roses and lilies he drew from the gardens of his patroness, the Empress Joséphine, at Malmaison, outside Paris. Reproductions of these fine prints exist in huge quantities and even originals are not hard to come by. Moreover, botanical drawings and prints are still being made in the late 20th century.

Of course, such prints and drawings were not intended to be hung on walls, but they look very handsome indeed when well framed. The current taste is to treat them as if they were watercolours, with moulded silver- or gold-leaf frames and mounts dressed with wash lines or even marbled paper borders. Whole groups, close hung, are especially effective – but only if work of the same period or artist is displayed together. Otherwise, black and white woodcuts from before the 16th century, framed in black, are strong enough for early interiors.

It was not long before plant portraits found their way onto other objects, especially in the 18th century when interest in the scientific study of the natural world was intense (the Swedish botanist Carl Linnaeus created a uniform system for the classification and naming of plants in the 1750s). Coincidentally, this was the golden age of European porcelain. Notable was the set of red anchor Chelsea plates named after Sir Hans Sloane, whose collection founded the British Museum in London. These were decorated with botanical paintings along with moths, butterflies and other insects. Portraits on other plates and dishes were sometimes less precise, but throughout the factories of Europe porcelain was being hand-painted with exact copies of roses, convolvulus, tulips, primulas and auriculas. Linnaeus himself had a Chinese teaset specially painted with his own flower, *Linnaea borealis*. By the 1760s craftsmen had begun modelling flowers in the round; for example, in Germany Meissen made vases studded with three-dimensional blooms.

From porcelain, botanical decoration descended to pottery. The British manufacturer Josiah Wedgwood was in the forefront. His brown-printed earthenware plate, made in 1806, takes water-lily flowers and leaves from botanical drawings. Early Wedgwood was very similar in style to the soft-paste porcelain it copied, but by the late 18th century the creamware had begun to develop characteristic floral border patterns of vine leaves, roses, carnations and honeysuckle, among others. These were the direct precursors of modern mass-production china patterns, which generally rely solely on a border or perhaps a small decoration in the middle of the piece. Another development was the all-over pattern, printed usually in blue. Huge floral bouquets, trailing rose borders, Chinese and Indian landscapes, even the famous willow pattern, arrived on British dining tables during the 19th century.

Josiah Wedgwood was also a pioneer in his policy of commissioning fine and decorative artists to design his plates. Factories had previously kept their own painters. Starting with sculptor John Flaxman's 18th-century vases in the antique style, the company went on to hire Emile and Thérèse Lessore in the 19th century and Eric Ravilious and Arnold Machin in the earlier 20th century, commissioning them to create both figures and designs.

The use of artists, designers and potters as freelances still goes on. A current trend has been to commission well-known ceramic designers to create pieces for small production runs. Modern work seems to favour bright, all-over patterns, perhaps because designers are reacting against the formal borders of the 19th-century and the neat graphics of the 1930s. Such all-over designs are good news for those who want to fill their bowls with lavender or potpourri because the earlier painted bouquets were far too beautiful to cover.

Potpourri should be made and used with care. The 18th-century housewife would make her own toward the end of summer when the flowers became full blown and fully scented. And we should too. A 19th-century book of druggists' receipts in my library gives a charming recipe for French potpourri. "Take the petals of the pale and red roses, pinks, violets, moss

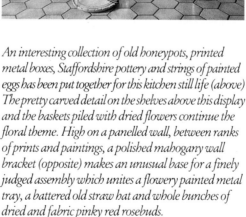

An interesting collection of old honeypots, printed metal boxes, Staffordshire pottery and strings of painted eggs has been put together for this kitchen still life (above) The pretty carved detail on the shelves above this display and the baskets piled with dried flowers continue the floral theme. High on a panelled wall, between ranks of prints and paintings, a polished mahogany wall bracket (opposite) makes an unusual base for a finely judged assembly which unites a flowery painted metal tray, a battered old straw hat and whole bunches of dried and fabric pinky red rosebuds.

rose, orange flower, lily of the valley, acacia flowers, clove-gilliflowers, mignonette, heliotrope, jonquils and with a small proportion of the flowers of myrtle, balm, rosemary and thyme; spread them out for some days and as they become dry, put them into a jar with alternate layers of dry salt, mixed with orris powder till the vessel is full. Close it for a month, then stir the whole up and moisten with rose water." Orrisroot – the powder of the rhizome of *Iris florentina* – is available from some pharmacies and herbalists. But, although recipes can be followed slavishly, it is more exciting to create an individual potpourri which will make a house memorable.

Pomanders are of much earlier origin but (apart from their use against the bubonic plague) the intention was the same. Hung in rooms, cupboards and closets, the spiced oranges would scent the air of Tudor houses. Sir Hugh Plat in his *Delights for Ladies* (1602), one of the first recipe books ever published in England, gives instruction on how to make "A Sweet and Delicate Pomander". But this recipe is so complex that it would be impossible to follow. Mrs Edward Neville, writing in the 1920s, suggests making pomanders of bitter Seville oranges; the fruit were first thoroughly dried by hanging them in nets in a warm kitchen or over a fire and then densely stuck with cloves.

The old cookbooks are full of ideas for using flowers. Georgina, Countess of Dudley, writing in 1909, proposes "A delicious bath when elder flowers are in blossom", in which the flowers are simply covered with boiling water, left to stand a few hours and the whole mixture then added to the bath. Much earlier, in 1753, *The Compleat Housewife* by one E. Smith suggests sweet bags for linen created from orrisroot, sweet calamus, cypress root, dried lemon and orange peel, dried roses, coriander, nutmeg and clove added to leaves of marjoram, orange and walnut and lavender flowers, all dried, rubbed and mixed with cotton perfumed "with essences" before being put into a silk bag among the linen.

Of course, flowers can also be eaten. In 1669 Sir Kenelm Digby, son of one of those executed with Guy Fawkes in the Gunpowder Plot, recommends a "sucket" or pastille of mallow stalks and a conserve of roses, adding, "Dr. Bacon useth to make a pleasant julep of this Conserve of roses by putting a good

spoonful of it into a large drinking glass upon which squeeze the juyce of a Limon, and clip in unto it a little of the yellow rinde...and adding to it, little by little a glass of Spring-water." Delicious. Constance Spry, writing during World War II, speaks about elderflower fritters, rose jam, hawthorn-flower brandy and sugar scented with rosemary or lavender flowers.

Flowers are put into salads too. Mrs Leyel, in a recipe of 1925, adds chrysanthemum flowers to a salad of potatoes, prawns, artichokes and egg, and tosses nasturtium leaves and flowers with lettuce. She also candies primroses, makes wine of cowslips and daisies, marmalade of violets and an omelette of salsify flowers. Even better, she adds rose petals to ice cream.

Like the making of pomanders, the art of drying flowers has not changed much over the centuries. No doubt our medieval ancestors were as likely to press especially lovely blooms as we are now. The preferred procedure today is between sheets of blotting paper under the carpet whereas then they used fabric (paper being a luxury). The technique of preserving a fresh flower in fine, dry sand which is then baked is probably as ancient, if not more so. The use of glycerine is more recent but was certainly known in the 19th century. Today, as then, great branches of beech leaves can survive for many weeks if they are first preserved in water mixed with glycerine.

Other flowers can be preserved by the age-old method of hanging them in a dry, heated room. Today's dried flower arrangers have all the world to choose from (not necessarily a good thing) with such oddities as lotus seedheads, Nevada cactus stalks and twisted Japanese willow branches now available in many specialist florists' shops. Extraordinarily lifelike silk flowers come from the East too and available in every major city in the West are whole preserved trees – palms and ficus, for example – so that any lightless interior can have its giant specimens. But these, like dried flowers, can quickly look tired unless they are dusted regularly. Nor are dried flowers appropriate for the spring. When the first snowdrops appear, a tiny nosegay of spring flowers is always preferable.

A recent variation on the dried flower theme is the abandoning of vases. It hardly takes great understanding to realize that dried flowers need no water, and designers have been strewing vast bunches on top of wardrobes and cupboards, lying them in willow baskets on flagged floors or on landings. Another

A selection of antique and reproduction floral pottery, made in England and in Continental Europe. Some pieces have decorative borders with featured motifs and some have all-over patterns. Blue and white pottery for the table has been popular since the 17th century. This is largely, I suspect, because food looks so good on it. For the key to the pieces, see page 184.

innovation has been to weave dried flowers into topiary shapes or to plant them in small terracotta pots for formal effects.

Papier mâché ware can also make a very decorative contribution to the floral scheme. The black backgrounds add solidity to a room dependent on flowery patterns, while being, of course, floral themselves. Papier mâché was first developed in the mid-18th century and restricted to objects suited to the generally fragile nature of the material, such as decorative trays, hand-painted in gold with delicate flower sprays. But in the 1820s, papier mâché furniture began to be made and a way of decorating it with inlaid mother-of-pearl was discovered. By the time of the Great Exhibition at Crystal Palace in London in 1851, the leading British manufacturer, Jennens and Bettridge, had ventured into full-sized chairs, pedestal tables and even a three-seater sofa (now at the Victoria and Albert Museum), its back painted with bouquets of flowers. A bed was also exhibited, made with brass mounts and highly decorative gilded swags surrounding painted and inlaid flowers. But this was a cheat because the papier mâché is on an iron base. Papier mâché was made in huge quantities and large amounts still exist. Since it is innately 19th century in style, it was very much out of fashion until the 1970s, but now it is sought after and there are antique dealers who specialize in it. The more extravagant pieces command high prices, but curiously the technique has not yet been revived.

Equally sought after today, and equally of their time, are the black tin or tole trays which copied papier mâché styles. Rather more practical than the originals, these have been reproduced and even reworked in more modern designs, as has tole ware generally. The term covers tin-plated objects made in Britain, France and the United States which can be plain japanned black, gilded with a simple border or covered with complex floral patterns and borders. Spice boxes, water jugs for the bath, fire buckets and coal scuttles were all made of tole. Smaller pieces and lamps with tole shades are often used today on occasional tables in the bedroom and floral living room, while the water jugs look most fetching in large bathrooms. Tole ware can be found at antique fairs specializing in the decorative arts (since they tend to be bought for decor rather than as collector's pieces), but original pieces are becoming rare. In general they are much finer than the reproductions, often being painted by hand and having the inimitable signs of wear.

Floral decoration on modern pottery tends toward abstraction and has been strongly influenced by movements in 20th-century painting. This selection comprises examples of potters working in the 1980s and 1990s. The exception is the papier mâché dish decorated with enormous daisy-like flowerheads (middle top). For the key to the pieces, see page 184.

Selecting a
Style

Period Themes

From the floral double-damasks of the Renaissance, as much at home on a bishop's back as on his walls, to the Baroque *repoussé* flowers on silver and the equally stylized dado friezes and flowered wallpaper of Art Nouveau in the late 19th century, period style is extraordinarily various. The earliest patterns were repetitive and often monochrome, but by the 17th century tapestries and carpets were highly coloured and continued so until the asymmetrical plasterwork, marquetry and gilding typical of Rococo arrived in the mid-18th century.

A hundred years later, the Industrial Revolution made multi-coloured, machine-made objects available to the less well-off, but poor design and execution led to a flood of garish products. By the 1880s a reaction was underway, notably with such designers as William Morris in England, Daniel Pabst in Philadelphia and Gustav Stickley in Syracuse, who looked back to the cottage and medieval traditions for inspiration. Today every period has its enthusiasts, and styles can be mixed if you group those which influenced one another together.

Lilies after Pierre Joseph Redouté decorate wall panels in a First Empire style salon in the Palais de Compiègne (opposite); stylized floral motifs appear on carpet, upholstery and mouldings. Colefax and Fowler chintz creates an up-to-date period look (overleaf). For fabrics above, see key on page 184.

Modern Themes

*T*oday's floral patterns have been greatly influenced by the work of 20th-century artists from the Impressionists and Fauves onward. Never before have patterns been so loosely, even splashily, formed, nor flowers rendered so impression-istically. Many of the best modern pieces are created by designers following closely the work of painters such as Raoul Dufy, Henri Matisse and Claude Monet or, more lately, Georgia O'Keeffe, Elizabeth Blackadder and David Hockney, and their patterns often have elements of the brushstroke and drawn pencil line about them, whether in fabric, porcelain, wallpaper or inlaid furniture. Their work may, in time, be as prized as originals by the 19th-century artists William Morris and Charles Rennie Mackintosh now are, so they are well worth collecting. Currently, patterns tend toward big, brash and bright floral designs in complete contrast to the ever-present, more traditional taste for flowers clearly displayed on a pale background. However, this style has now held sway for more than a decade and a reaction must soon be due.

The "beanstalks" which climb the walls and sloping ceilings of potter Mary Rose Young's English cottage (opposite) have a splashy immediacy typical of many modern floral designs, whereas the floral reference on the patterned floor is more oblique. For fabrics above, see key on page 184.

Faded Palette

"Faded" fabrics began to be created when decorators realized that it was impossible to achieve the authentic country-house look without swathes of faded old chintz at the window and on the sofa. The demand for authentically faded linen, chintz, tapestry and embroidery was outstripping supply and collectors were loathe to press prize pieces into use so fabric designers turned to re-creating new "old" fabrics. Based always on a background which looks as if it has been stained by tea – the colour old linen achieves with age – the patterns are toned down as though they have been bleached by the sun. Strong light quickly removes greens and yellows whereas red and some blues are more resistant so the faded fabrics come in gentle shades of rose-madder, green-brown, gray-beige and gray-blue. Virtually all the faded cottons and linens now available are in floral patterns, which have generally been copied or adapted from prints designed in the late 18th and 19th centuries, and "aged" wallpapers have more recently been created in the same mood, using authentic patterns and pale, dulled backgrounds.

Mixed to perfection, a charming collection of faded fabrics from the late Geoffrey Bennison (opposite): "All-Over Floral" (pink) on the walls and armchair, "Regular Rosevine" (purple) on the sofa and "English Oakleaf" on the tablecloth and cushions or pillows. For fabrics above, see key on page 184.

Bright Palette

We tend to think that 16th- and 17th-century houses were dark and dull but this is a misconception because many of the colours we see today have faded – the gilding goes brown, the vegetable-dyed tapestries lose their bright reds and the painting on rose and vine ceiling mouldings is dulled by varnish. But pieces of pottery survive to show us the brightness of Italian and Spanish maiolica, and carefully tended Chinese hangings and Indian inlays prove that, when they could get them, our ancestors loved bright colours. Bright florals remain just as popular today and, as then, contrasting primary shades are set on bright backgrounds, chrome-yellow being a favourite. But now the range of designs has widened from the exotic flowers of the 18th century to include more naturalistic portraits of roses, fuchsias and mingled herbaceous plants. Some pile pattern on pattern, the flowers themselves becoming backgrounds for other bright patterns. At the same time, porcelain factories such as Ginori in Italy and Limoges in France are reviving old designs. Such bold pieces look their best in bright, sunny rooms.

Bright florals such as Sanderson's lemon-based "Beauchamp" (opposite) enjoy the contrast of strong, plainer patterns. But a Chinoiserie design on the walls of a New York apartment (overleaf) works well with muted drapes and the pale tones of tapestry. For fabrics above, see key on page 184.

Monochrome Florals

$\mathcal{M}$ulticoloured pieces can hide a multitude of design sins, but monochrome floral patterns are generally meticulous, finely detailed and graphically elegant. Before the Industrial Revolution, it could take weeks to complete the printing on fabric of even one colour so monochrome patterns on a white or cream background were obviously the simplest, and cheapest, to create. But, while such fabrics lost vigour through lack of colour, the care taken over the patterns made up for it. Fashionable artists were commissioned to create complex landscapes, floral bouquets or concoctions of boughs, blooms and birds, and fine copper was engraved to print them. As wallpaper grew fashionable, these prints were adapted to suit, later appearing on formal screens and hat boxes. The monochrome pattern was also typical of early 19th-century pottery, which was adorned with vines or roses, and of tinware and treen boxes. High-quality design techniques continue today, especially in French wallpapers and bone china. Monochrome florals adapt to life in a cottage or castle, to town or country.

Monochrome schemes must be carefully planned if they are to maintain interest. The extraordinary detail of blue toile *(opposite), richly garlanded with fruit and foliage, never disappoints and note how the non-figurative patterns elsewhere emphasize its delicacy. For fabrics above, see key on page 185.*

Rainbow Florals

These florals take their lead from the best kind of cottage garden with its riot of colour, a mix which somehow always avoids any hint of a clash. A gloriously spontaneous muddle of pansies, poppies, irises, tulips, roses, daisies, marigolds, in season and out, the flowers seem to break all the rules of "good" design. And yet, behind the apparent chaos is discipline – a dark or strong background tone which holds the design together or the colours themselves cleverly grouped so that they contrive to create a pattern within a pattern. Such designs, with their violent colour contrasts, come from a multiplicity of sources – from Eastern chintz, Moorish inlays, Art Nouveau tiles and papers and from the bold colours of the 20th-century Fauve and Blaue Reiter schools of painting. Unlike the bright patterns which look their best in the sun, these do well in dark country-cottage living rooms or in sloping attic bedrooms in town or country. They are essentially relaxed and casual in feeling, emphatically not designed for the sophistication of a grand townhouse or for a city apartment with pretensions to Modernism.

Pink and orange blooms riot against a dark background in a Dorma fabric which peps up the cool greens of a simple country bedroom (opposite). Individual colours from the duvet repeated in decorative objects around the room unify this lively scheme. For fabrics above, see key on page 185.

Small Patterns

*T*raditionally, small patterns were assigned to inferior positions in great houses: the basin and ewer, the lining to the damask drapes, the case-covers put over furniture when the family was away, the housekeeper's bedroom. This simple modesty is part of their charm. No swash was buckled in their creation, so the designs, while far from naive, speak directly to us. Their use for linings has been revived and, while housekeepers are an endangered species, small-patterned fabrics and wall-papers now adorn country cottages from the Pennines to the

Apennines and the Appalachians. Today their inspiration is drawn widely, from the paisleys of Provence, the delicate and tiny flowers embroidered on 18th-century dress silks, all-over architectural carvings of seaweed and sprig shapes, the patterns found around tole trays and the all-over prints on pretty 19th-century loving cups, ewers, chargers and jugs, marbled, stippled and printed with flowers. Against larger and louder flowers, they offer a complementary change of scale, and they are a delightful choice for bedrooms, childrens' rooms and for tables.

A tiny sprig-patterned wallpaper can create an instant period effect (opposite). In a room crowded with 19th-century detail it is a choice which pairs happily with the stylized floral patterns on the kelim thrown over the fireside table and the rug before the fire. For fabrics above, see key on page 185.

Large Patterns

Giant flowers are by no means a novelty in floral design. They were quite commonplace in the furniture, carving and fabrics of Renaissance Italy, and the Pre-Raphaelites encouraged giant blooms on everything from tiles to stained glass. But this century has proved unaccountably nervous of them until recently, when fabric designers such as Manuel Canovas recoloured and updated the giant bloom, taking inspiration from the silk damask designs of 14th-century Florence and 17th-century blackwork embroidery. Other designers followed the lead of Van Gogh's sunflowers and the blowsy poppies of the German painter Emil Nölde. Many designs seem to be painted with broad, almost casual brushstrokes, whereas others are outlined in black and then coloured in. Modern pottery, especially, has espoused the large bloom, which may cover an entire plate. The flowers themselves are usually those with large blooms in nature – peonies, hybrid clematis, tulips – or stylized shapes. Curiously, these huge designs seem at home both in traditional and Modernist settings – if the scale is right.

A large design works best where it has space to "breathe", as does this exotic 18th-century French fabric on the walls of a grand Parisian house (opposite). Note how it is tempered by cool gray-green paintwork which echoes the frame of the bucket chair. For fabrics above, see key on page 185.

Flowers in Bud

Floral designs that rely on the promise of things to come have long attracted the meticulous craftsmanship required for hand-painted porcelain and needlepoint. The flower in bud has an entirely different appeal to that of the flower in bloom; the tightly rolled petals may be a darker shade than when they unfurl and the delicate leaves which surround the bud contribute far more elegance of form than they do later. The most popular flower buds were those of the rose, fuchsia, carnation and convolvulus. These and many indeterminate buds were strewed over the backgrounds of pottery and porcelain to give an all-over pattern for more dramatic blooms; they appear similarly in tapestry, papier mâché and tinware. Buds were also highly popular for borders, whether of fabric or wallpaper. Today's patterns owe much to them, as well as to 18th-century plaster-work and dress silks and 19th-century printed pottery and paper. Small in scale and full of charm, they are at their best in bedroom, boudoir or cottage. They can also be wittily used to complement fabrics with the same flower in full bloom.

Fabrics dotted with rosebuds will easily create a reassuringly pretty bedroom; this charming combination (opposite) is by Dorma. The bud motif set on narrow stripes is a popular pattern in floral decor and owes much to 18th-century English and French dress fabrics. For fabrics above, see key on page 185.

Flowers in Bloom

Most floral designs show plenty of open flowers, but there are some which take an obvious delight in really flouncy blossom. Delicate blooms such as the poppy, whose petals spring crinkled from tight green buds, and the clematis and passionflower with their wide, flat faces are the type which encourage this kind of ebullience in designers. For ebullient these designs for chargers, trays and rugs certainly are – brightly coloured, more than lifesize and exuberantly splashed on contrasting backgrounds. Their blowsiness appeals especially to the young and these patterns are very much of the 20th century. Frequently, in defiance of all tenets of taste, big blooms are bundled together in great ranges of colour – purple, ultramarine, scarlet, lemon and acid green – which somehow suit the style. Nor can I detect much discipline in the best examples of their use – perhaps you just need the perfect "eye". Indeed, there is something cheerfully Post-Modernist about the humour with which the bold primary colours are balanced. The fabrics are as at home on a country sofa as they are in a city apartment.

Generous bouquets of muted full-blown flowers are very much at home in the bedroom, as in a Dorma fabric lavishly trimmed with cotton lace (opposite) and in an attic room (overleaf), where multicoloured blooms disguise the awkwardly sloping ceiling. For fabrics above, see key on page 185.

Botanical Designs

Detailed plant portraits, showing leaf, stem, bloom, bud, seedhead and root all in one picture, have been featured on fabrics and ceramics for more than 200 years. With a genuine public interest in the new science of botany such 18th-century illustrations quickly made the transition from books to framed prints to fabrics. Plants which created crazes when first introduced – tulips, parrot and striped, vari-coloured auriculas and primulas, plus those discovered during the voyages of exploration – became prime targets for designers and these subjects are enjoying a revival today. They appear on fabrics, needlepoint cushions or pillows and even place mats, with the plant portrait often set in a cartouche surrounded by a strong, dark colour. Porcelain still maintains the style begun by the Chelsea and Copenhagen factories when Chelsea painted plates with Sir Hans Sloane's discoveries and the Danish botanist Linnaeus was celebrated with the Flora Danica pattern. The modern botanicals contrive to be both assertive in their strong designs and traditional in their copying of 18th-century prints.

Nina Campbell's "Bagatelle" (opposite) is an unusual update of the botanical print. Accurate portraits of old roses and primulas within a traditional cartouche are set on a two-tone abstract pattern which has almost the naive quality of a child's potato print. For fabrics above, see key on page 186.

Diagrammatic Designs

*M*any of the earliest flower designs found in decoration – on Egyptian gold jewellry, ceiling mouldings in Greek temples, dado frescoes in Roman villas and borders around Mughal pictures – made no attempt to define which flowers were being depicted. Patterns were created from what was recognizably a flower shape without specific distinguishing features. Later, the designers of Renaissance damasks, 17th-century tapestries, 18th-century sprigs and even Art Deco patterns used the flower as an abstract symbol. One advantage of the style is that flexible repeating patterns, large and small, can be created without the awkward limitations of realism. Another, as architects have found, is that formalized flower patterns can be linked or backed very effectively by abstract stems and swags. And designers everywhere have discovered that the diagrammatic flower will adapt to their medium: palmettes on furniture, acanthus leaves on candelabra, anthemions on silver sauceboats and scrolling foliage around the borders of porcelain dishes. It is a style found in every decorating movement that ever existed.

"Palmiers" (opposite) is a diagrammatic design by Comoglio, derived and adapted from an 18th-century Marseilles pattern book. This handsome linen and cotton fabric works well on a French sofa of the same period because it does not overwhelm the piece. For fabrics above, see key on page 186.

Inspiration from India

*M*ost of the commonly used floral designs available today are based on "chintz", brightly coloured cotton prints imported into Europe from India and Persia from the end of the 17th century (indeed the French term is *persienne*) until England's cotton mills started to send them back – cheaper. In France and Scotland the motifs of Kashmir weaves were soon copied on shawls, and modern Western fabric designers still pay homage to earlier Indian craftsmen, not only by copying their colourful designs, but in the names they give them, such as "Malabar",

"Indore" and "Seringapatam". Indian motifs are equally common on china – the Indian tree of life pattern is used nearly as often as the willow pattern – while small papier mâché, *pietra dura* and painted wooden pieces are all clearly influenced by the bright inlay work of the sub-continent. There are even signs that Benares brassware, its patterns stamped on everything from octagonal trays to cigarette boxes, is enjoying a come-back. Because of this long tradition in our homes, Indian-inspired designs are at ease with virtually every style and period.

Brilliant colouring and all-over patterns denote the influence of India as defined by Designers Guild (opposite). The green paisley wallpaper is the stable element in a room where gilded crimson curtains or drapes are the backdrop for a strong, paisley-influenced hanging. For fabrics above, see key on page 186.

Inspiration from China

Today, as throughout history, the Chinese prefer to embroider or paint their patterns freehand rather than print them, perhaps because symmetry has never been important in Chinese design. Modern Chinoiserie takes its inspiration from several sources – from the gorgeously embroidered robes and banners of the Imperial family and their mandarins, from the free-flowing calligraphy on scrolls and pottery, and from the curious angles and carving on their inlaid, hardwood furniture. The natural growth of bamboo, both its leaves and jointed stems,

is yet another source. These patterns found their way onto fabrics, Delft vases, prints, *faux* bamboo furniture and "Chinese" Chippendale or Duncan Phyfe chairs. Chinoiserie has been popular as long as tea-drinking in the West and shows no sign of decline. Colours remain the traditional colours of Chinese porcelain – blue and white or *famille rose*, *verte*, *jaune* or *noire* with accents of peony-pink and celadon. These are sophisticated designs, drawn directly from the world's oldest and, arguably, finest artists and craftsmen, and should be treated as such.

A passion for Delft Chinoiserie determined the scheme for this bedroom at the Chateau de Morsan, France (opposite).
Splendid examples of the blue and white pottery deck almost every surface and the owner has hand-painted the walls
with motifs derived from it. For fabrics above, see key on page 186.

Choosing a
Colour Theme

The Red Anthology

A charming French provincial bedroom (opposite) created by the fabric firm Comoglio for a grand Parisian townhouse that was once an ambassador's residence. The walls are covered with "Roses Anciennes", a dainty pattern in shades of red on a pale ground; the quilt of vine leaves and grapes is "Petit Mouton" (red), lined with "Apt" to match the undersheet.

A 19th-century French print of an old rose, the crimson 'Duchesse de Dino' (left). Red rose petals have always been prized ingredients for potpourri and some recipes even require fragrant rose leaves. The secret is never to gather them after rain and always to dry them thoroughly before beginning work. For the key to the fabrics on the previous pages, see page 186.

Of all the flowers of the world, the rose is queen. Its blooms, from the palest pink to the darkest crimson, cover the entire red spectrum and its history is magnificent. Roses grew in the gardens of the legendary Phrygian King Midas, were painted on the walls of the palace of Knossos, near Heraklion, in Crete, and appear in the beautiful frescoes which were uncovered at Pompeii. In fact, the only flower the Greeks seemed to value in a leaf-dominated world was the rose, which, Herodotus said, could be found, wild and sweet-smelling, in Macedonia. Even in the 4th century BC, coins were being minted with flowers as decoration. At Rhodes, for example, one was stamped with a half-opened rose and its buds – others were more mundane, having fig leaves or celery stalks for decoration.

In Classical art the rose represents love as well as Venus, the goddess of love, a symbolism to which Sandro Botticelli, the 15th-century Italian Renaissance painter, refers in *The Birth of Venus*. By contrast, in Christian art the flower is used as a symbol of the Virgin Mary and purity. The word "rosary" itself derives

from the rose, and nine saints carry roses as their emblem. However, Classical and Christian influences do sometimes work together. In architecture, for example, the inspiration for the stylized roses above some church confessionals, symbolizing confidentiality, can be traced back to the Greek myth in which Cupid, Venus' son, gave the god of silence a rose to keep quiet about his mother's love life.

Le Roman de la Rose, an epic ballad poem written in France during the 13th century and the central text of the courtly love tradition, begins with the allegorical dream of a poet searching for his lady's love, symbolized by a rose. From that time on, to give roses, especially red ones, has signified romance and love.

As heraldic badges, roses symbolized the Houses of York (white) and Lancaster (red), which fought over the English monarchy in the Wars of the Roses during the 15th century. The white rose of the victorious House of York became eventually the emblem of England. Today, without the rose, from tightly furled bud to dying bloom, English country-house style would lose its identity. On wallpaper or chintz, sewn onto needlepoint pillows or as a scented potpourri, the flower of England is the flower of English style.

England has no monopoly on the flower though. Throughout northern Europe Gothic cathedrals celebrated nature with brightly coloured rose windows and that at Chartres is probably the biggest ever depiction of a single flower. In French Renaissance tapestries virgins and unicorns gambol on fields of silk or wool roses. The Genoese silks and Spanish leather hangings of the 16th and 17th centuries stylized the rose in their borders and cartouches and 18th-century porcelain makers from Meissen to Sèvres began a love affair with the flower which has never ended. Roses also appear as a stylized motif in the Art Nouveau movement – in houses designed by Glasgow architect Charles Rennie Mackintosh in the late 19th century and in the austere work of the Vienna Secessionists in the early 20th century.

Curiously, the rose, which is often represented as the European flower par excellence, probably came from the Middle East, although one variety was certainly known in China. However, the Chinese have always given their allegiance to that other great bloom of the red spectrum, the peony. This gloriously blowsy flower was growing in Chinese gardens 500 years before Christ and, by the 11th century AD, during the Sung dynasty, was appearing on porcelain and in paintings. Europeans learned to love the peony in porcelain long before they saw one in reality. The plant proved so difficult to keep alive on the long voyage home that the first flowers

A hand-coloured 19th-century print of Fuchsia grommiana. *The genus was first introduced into Europe from Central and South America and the Pacific islands during the 19th century and quickly became immensely popular.*

did not appear in the West until 1789. The peony is the flower which typifies Chinese *famille rose* (*rose* here meaning "pink") porcelain. Its glowing, recurved petals also appear on Chinese silk embroidery, incised in celadon porcelain, drawn with flowing calligraphic brushstrokes and painted by emperors. If modern fabric makers want to give their designs an Oriental touch, it is the peony they choose.

Gentler-hued plants in shades of pink and peach, mostly native to the Mediterranean shores, have traditionally been used to decorate homes. The clove pink or carnation from Spain has perfumed rooms with its spicy scent since the reign of the Roman Emperor Augustus, and many centuries later it was taken up by the weavers of Paisley shawls in Scotland, where special varieties were bred. The common pink was beloved by the monks of

medieval Britain and today, more than 400 years since the dissolution of the monasteries, this tiny plant may be found rooting in ruined abbeys.

The shy, shell-pink blooms of the lovely wild cyclamen, far removed from the florist's inbred monsters, can still be found twined with ivy in Italian glades. This favourite of early herbalists is also native to Iran and Greece. The frail and hairy anemone, another native of Italy, was so treasured that a legend grew up that the scarlet flower which bloomed on the Campo Santo, beside Pisa's Duomo, was brought back from the Holy Land by returning Crusaders. It is also a symbol of death. In Greek mythology its scarlet flowers sprouted where Adonis' blood fell.

Adonis is said to symbolize the vegetative cycle and in another fascinating Classical/Christian parallel the anemone is often shown growing at the foot of the cross in paintings that depict Christ's crucifixion.

Scarlet poppies also became a sombre reminder of death this century when, like blood, they sprang from the war-scarred fields of Flanders during World War I. The flower remains the symbol of regret for that slaughter. In Classical mythology the poppy was the attribute of Hypnos, the Greek god of sleep, and his Roman counterpart, Morpheus, god of dreams, who wore the flower in his hair. In both cases, the association with the flower is a reference to the opium obtained from the plant. It was also the flower of Ceres, the Roman goddess of agriculture, because it is so often seen growing in wheat fields.

Several magnificent red flowers are native to the Americas. The fuchsia, a drooping beauty whose petal skirts are at their best in hanging baskets, became one of the main ingredients in floral fabrics in the 19th century. The zinnia and the dahlia feature less frequently as design motifs, perhaps because of their associations with the violent civilization of the Aztec Indians.

Finally, to a plant well-loved by gardeners – the pelargonium or pot geranium in all its many forms. Ivy-leaved and sharply scented, it is a fond reminder of sun-baked Mediterranean doorsteps, where it blooms all summer in terracotta pots. From puce to vermilion to white-striped crimson, clustered together they prove that nature can be startlingly successful with adventurous colour combinations. But bear in mind that the artificial world of carpets and ceramics, wallpaper and fabric is a great deal less forgiving.

The warm and cool tones of the red spectrum combine for the handsome rhododendron blooms on the upholstery and curtains or drapes in this traditional townhouse living room.

Conflicting florals – on the curtains or drapes, the sofa and on the carpet – are reconciled by plainer, toning fabrics: pinky red on the chairs and tartan on cushions or pillows and tablecloth.

A clever eye and confidence are required for this strong visual statement. Note the repeat of the huge, complex red floral pattern on the tables and screen, the flower frieze above the dado and the necessary boldness of the silvered mirror and the Chinese jars.

The faded reds of the old roses on the sofa fabric defer to the stronger red on the diagrammatic foliage wallpaper, whereas the toning colours of the carpet mix diagrammatic bouquets and sprigs. Red rosettes on the picture hangers repeat the floral theme.

RED ARRANGEMENTS

Roses, as well as being the star flower in decor, must also be that most used in flower arrangements. But forget that cliché of a dozen long-stemmed florist's crimson blooms, so stiff and regimented they might be plastic, and concentrate instead on those grown by gardeners. The old-fashioned shrub roses are especially good for arrangements, I think, because of the shape of their buds and the way that the petals of the open flower cluster and curve. Each variety – and there are hundreds – has individuality. Even small arrangements on tabletops or dressing tables repay detailed observation. These blooms ask only the minimum from the arranger – put them into a simple vase and stand back to admire – and in autumn or the fall, look out for roses with bright crimson, vase-shaped hips.

There are plenty of other red and pink flowers which do well in arrangements. For example, all the herbaceous peonies are wonderfully lush and will flower freely if the plants are well fed. The pink and dark crimson ones so favoured in cottage gardens are especially useful. Shrubby rhododendrons do not mind being picked and, as well as the pinky-purple common variety now rampant in many temperate-zone woodlands, there are beautiful early pale pink flowers and, among the smaller species, one with rosy pink bellflowers surrounded by coppery leaves that looks excellent alongside dark oak furniture.

The summer herbaceous border plants offer a huge choice of colourful flowers, from the complicated pink, orange, cream and apricot heads of hybrid lupins (wonderful on a hall table) to the delicate flowers of love-lies-bleeding, whose drooping sprays hang so beautifully, or the architectural form of the purple-pink martagon or Turk's cap lily.

The cottage-garden flowers – such as sweet william, pink and apricot honeysuckle and even the kniphofia – are midsummer favourites and best contrasted with bright green leaves. I also like little nosegays of pinks, crimson daisies or bell heathers. Though there are not many pink or red spring bulbs, thankfully the deep pink lily-type flowers of the nerine turn up in autumn (fall) at a thin time for arrangers. Nor should you forget that winter standby, the red-barked dogwood.

A highly complex display of flowers and berries (opposite) cheers a winter room, repeating and intensifying the reds in drapes, holly garlands and fruit. Lilies, single chrysanthemums, the pinky dried heads of hydrangeas and glossy evergreens contribute to the effect. Arrangements of this sort owe much to the influence of the English flower arranger Constance Spry, whose taste held sway until the 1970s. To say that such displays are becoming unfashionable is not to deny their beauty, but more natural arrangements can be equally appealing: (top left) translucent red guelder-rose berries and statice with a hint of purple combine in a Mason's ironstone bowl; (top right) old roses from the softer end of the red spectrum are perked up by a touch of yellow and gray-green spikes of rosemary; (bottom left) the gentle purples of valerian and buddleia blend in the foreground, while 19th-century rhyton vases hold tiny nosegays of freesia; and (bottom right) red peonies provide a backdrop for bowls laden with fruit.

RED LIVING ROOMS

*L*iving rooms which rely on the red spectrum for their colouring can achieve surprising variety. At one end of the shade card, if you use crimson, claret or Etruscan red, the room will be mysterious, enclosed. It becomes a place designed for night-time, made exotic with sealing-wax red lilies or languorous orchids, and a space which is both grand and totally urban. Use the other end of the spectrum and you create a room in total contrast – a living room for the daytime, for flinging the windows wide and letting the scent of roses flood in. This room is decked in the pretty pinks that match the inside of a conch shell; these are the colours of country-house chintz and the roses English 18th-century painter Thomas Gainsborough's frilled ladies clutched to lend themselves delicacy.

Between these two extremes, what wonderful choice the red flowers can offer: shocking-pink petunia shades, the vibrant vermilion tones of the pelargonium or pot geranium, the strong, orangey reds of tropical plants like strelitzia and the purple of bourgainvillea, all of which work best in strong sunlight. Then there are the duller earth-based terracotta reds that come alive with the help of bright dogwood bark, pink pottery urns full of flowers or huge tubs of dark scarlet leaves.

Every English country-house living room, even in the grandest house, has one essential feature – the huge comfy sofa, big enough for whole tribes of dogs or children and consequently loose-covered in a dirt-defying rosy chintz. Was it the need to cope with muddy paws that led to England's love affair with splashy prints? Naturally, the sofa will be accompanied by several equally floppy armchairs, often covered in a different floral chintz – great big scarlet peonies on a shiny black ground perhaps, or those sketchy flourishes of leaves and ribbons in dark pink on a lighter ground.

Such rooms also often feature the figurative flowers of Aubusson-type carpets or squared 19th-century needlepoint rugs. Luckily, since 18th-century French carpets are in dwindling supply, new copies have recently come on the market and can be made to fit both the floor area and the colour plan.

Traditionally, these rooms are the home of the prettier paintings: landscapes, flower studies in oil, even 18th- and 19th-century Berlin woolwork pictures of children in garlands of flowers. The United States pioneered the use of mounds of needlepoint cushions or pillows – a style that has now spread worldwide, helped by the late Duchess of Windsor – and so roses, pink-striped tulips and poppies vie with embroidered

Red florals need not overwhelm, as the subdued pattern on a pair of armchairs (above left) and the delightful Comoglio design "Roses Anciennes" (above right) both demonstrate. Toning trim raises the armchairs above the purely traditional, whereas every element in the other room can receive equal attention.

The grand proportions of a French chateau (opposite) accept the challenge of a magnificent red print but with walls, windows and sofa covers in the same pattern the other floral elements need careful planning. The plant portraits, on the walls and on the sofa cushions or pillows, have an almost naive clarity.

*The faded palest pink roses on the sofa do not try to
compete with the velvety real blooms in the glass jug
(see detail, opposite) and that is why the mixture works.
The stylized red floral designs on tapestry chairs, pillows
and rug are equally muted and even the little table
before the sofa is painted with flowers and fruit.*

mottoes and homilies. Some of the most charming pink porcelain will find its way here too – little Derby spill vases with hand-painted pinks or French *faïence* candlesticks decorated with naive pink geraniums and turned into charming lamps, topped with flowery shades.

Because these pretty bits and pieces are unassuming they will suit the smallest cottage living room just as happily. Nor do they need the boost of antique furniture. You can create a relaxed mood by the subtle use of a range of well-designed red and pink fabrics, wallpapers and knicknacks. Quality is all important – anything badly designed or awkwardly coloured or out of keeping can wreck this kind of inspired clutter. But a charmingly painted rose on a little dish or a carefully stitched modern sampler in a distressed frame can be effective at minimum cost.

Although unadulterated rosy prettiness works perfectly in town, many urbanites prefer stronger bones for their rooms, especially in the formal setting of an 18th-century townhouse. Here the symmetry of a French or Italian salon, with orangey apricot or madder-pink silk-damask walls figured with stylized tulips or irises and furnished with dainty gray and gilt upholstered, straight-backed chairs, evokes a calm contrast with life on the busy streets outside. Stylized big-repeat designs in bright scarlet and green, or self-coloured peach silks, look wonderful on the padded backs and seats.

Somewhere between these two approaches lies the romantic look of the Swedish Gustavian style. This is the French salon transformed by northern light and simplicity. Pretty tiled stoves, wooden floors painted with garlands of meadow flowers and walls hung with canvas hand-embroidered with sprays of roses, pink daisies, handsome poppies and mauvy-red hydrangeas are all typical of this highly fashionable look. Incidentally, such a style adapts easily to all of northern Europe and the more northerly states of North America. In the southern states you need look no farther than the Manship House in Jackson, Mississippi. Garnet silk drapes are echoed by rich crimson table-cloths and a carpet of roses on a grass-green ground. The whole scheme is saved from oppressiveness by a careful lack of clutter and a grisaille wallpaper of exotic foliage.

Whatever style you choose, the secret of success lies in the skill with which the fabrics, furniture, wallpaper and objects are selected and mixed. A red scheme makes more demands than any other because the colour spectrum is so vast and clashes so easy. Pick just one tone and stick to it; then vary the shade. The more formal the scheme, the fewer the mix of patterns (except self-coloured ones). The relaxed country style, on the other hand, encourages a veritable riot of pattern. Every cushion or pillow a different rose, but if the decorator's eye is cunning (and secretly disciplined) the riot will be tamed to a carnival.

RED DINING ROOMS & KITCHENS

*I*t seems a pity that the red dining room has fallen into such disfavour. Like the brightest and best flowers in the red spectrum, red rooms are challenging, vibrant, fizzing with fun and action. The time has come to revive them. Red can be adapted to today's two very different styles of eating: the formal dining room – a place of table settings, silver candlesticks and carefully considered nosegays, a room at its best after dark – or the family kitchen, awash with children and pets, a friendly range settled on terracotta tiles, where real friends are invited to eat.

In the first, you eat off porcelain plates, painted with 18th-century flower patterns. In the second, the dishes are of hearty pottery, hand-painted like the first, but in the peasant tradition; roses and artless bouquets bloom on heavy white glazes, and handles are formed from pink twined stems.

Traditionally, the formal dining room has Persian carpets underfoot, sprinkled with stylized flowers, but every other detail is kept sombre, even severe. Clever decorators can get away with draping plain chairs, but in unskilled hands such flouncing becomes disastrous. Equally, although an exuberant wallpaper can work, it should be tempered with banks of sober pictures: silhouettes, perhaps, family portraits certainly or, if you are lucky enough to find them, bold and beautiful oils of huge, contrived flower arrangements. The table should be laid with matching flowered porcelain and an elegant silver centrepiece. This can be filled with a multiplicity of different floral arrangements, from tiny glasses, each holding a pink or purple orchid, to winter confections of dried materials. Stems of orangey willow or red cornus are a modern fashion, as are sometimes rather self-conscious fruit and vegetable arrangements.

The family kitchen has far more vitality. Great dressers can be stacked with collections of pretty plates. They do not need to be sets, but a controlling theme is important. Try a madder-pink transfer pattern, the great bright roses splashed over Scottish Weymss ware or modern hand-painted peasant pottery from Italy, Spain or Portugal. White enamel mugs stencilled with roses or chrysanthemums can hang from hooks on the dresser's sides, along with pretty pink spongeware decorated with cherubs and rosebuds. All are brought down for great family parties, when a bright red embroidered cloth from the Balkans is draped over the kitchen table and everyone serves themselves from a big French soup tureen, its white glaze garlanded with sprigs of pink Mediterranean flowers.

Of course, there is no reason why a large house cannot contain both rooms. The formalities of pheasant and port are best enjoyed in a dining room, its sombre reds touched with gleams of gold in the candlelight, whereas the tricks of eating pasta and tomato sauce demand the family kitchen.

Tuscany in London: the plum and ochre fabrics on the chairs, heavily tasselled curtains or drapes and tablecloth are in traditional Italian floral damask patterns which echo the colours in the old terracotta-painted walls and the real terracotta-tiled floor. In daylight in midsummer the yellower tones of terracotta are apparent, but in candlelight the redder tones will warm the diners, providing a subtle complement to the appealing austerity of this imaginative scheme.

RED BEDROOMS

*P*retty pinks and blush madder are the obvious choices when creating a flowery bedroom with a red colour scheme. And many decorators cannot wait to primp and swag a bedroom, using that most flattering of shades, the pale peach so beloved by Hollywood set designers. This is a style rarely enjoyed by those with more formal, less romantic tastes, but bedrooms are invariably more relaxed than other parts of the house and informality always creeps in somewhere – needlepoint rugs, crewelwork cushions or pillows strewn with blooms, neat bundles of linen tied with rose-embroidered satin ribbons, willow baskets filled with crimson paisley shawls or pomanders and lavender bags nestling among the hangers.

Comfortably at home in the bedroom are the French madder-pink fabrics known as *toiles de Jouy* and decked with rural bowers and Arcadian shepherdesses. These scenic cottons were also made in England and the United States, and everywhere antique pieces are now eagerly sought to swag four-poster beds, dress goosefeather pillows or spread over those low French screens that are so useful to hide mundane necessities.

Drawings from the 19th century show generous bedrooms hung with flowery pink curtains and beds covered with rose-printed quilts and cushions. Re-creating this kind of pretty room is one of the easier tasks for the floral decorator. The source material is so readily available and the period furniture, the actual fabrics, the embroideries and ornaments exist in large quantities and at not too disturbing prices. And, where they do not, shoals of designers are re-inventing them. Some of the prettiest

The curtains or drapes, bedhangings and cushions or pillows are all in the same red-rose Jane Churchill fabric (left), but note how the changes are rung with the immensely flattering pink linings on the bed and the dark red of the frilled trims. A single file of botanical prints, the table lamps and even the delicate bedside china continue the red flower theme. A matching wallpaper and bedcover in a charming pink and lime pattern are also a workable solution to the perennial problem of the bed's looming presence in a relatively small room (far left) which has been crammed with much-loved furniture and pictures.

modern-day rosy fabrics, tole lights, trays and vases are painted with full-blown herbaceous border plants copied by enthusiasts for the 19th century from old pattern books, and even Victorian-style tub chairs can be bought, deep-buttoned, to stand beside the glowing bedroom fireplace.

But red bedrooms need not evoke the flounce of a full-blown rose. The deep crimson of a formal floral damask, the colour of a cardinal's robe, when hung around a black oak bed will instantly conjure up the 17th century or the black precision of Italian Renaissance interiors. Or what of lacquer red – favourite colour of the legendary US *Vogue* editor, Diana Vreeland – or scarlet? Combine them with gold-backed Japanese Rimpa screens, their panels covered with brilliant crimson flowers, and an antique kimono embroidered with stylized chrysanthemums, casually thrown over scarlet or black satin sheets on a lacquered bed, to create a wicked mixture of the Far East and *fin-de-siècle* decadence. Use the same Oriental elements with *tatami* mats and a low, plain bed and all Western influence disappears. Add a single perfect spray of barely pink apple blossom in a thick-glazed porcelain vase and the room gains an Oriental serenity.

A different form of Minimalism is the ascetic approach: bare pink plaster walls, a campaign bed and a flowery rag rug on bare boards. This has the advantages of being frugal and also well suited to pokey old cottages. Or choose American colonial style, with painted floors, flower-patterned patchwork and gaudy china ewers. From English cottage to Italian primitive, the red spectrum allows infinite changes of pace and style: charming, spartan, sinful, *faux naïf*, rural or urban.

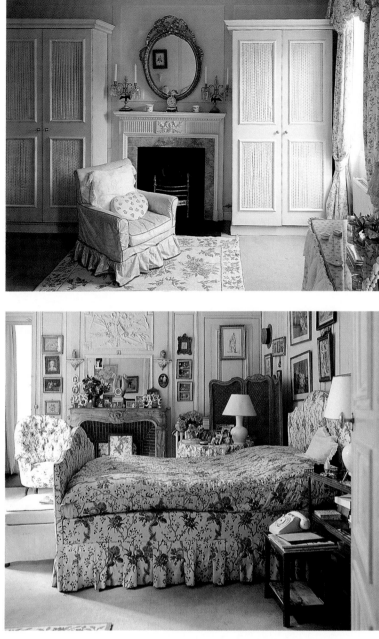

These elegant bedrooms both use the same scheme of restrained pastel walls, painted or panelled, as a calm background for busy yet pale fabrics in the red spectrum. Exquisite detail rewards the eye in the first room (left and top). There are charming flower portraits on the walls and floral designs in the lace on the dressing table, the bedcovering and the lamps, in the self-patterned upholstery, on the china and even the photograph frame by the bed. And note an interesting, subtle touch – a porcelain mug of blue blooms to turn aside a surfeit of sweetness. The other room (above) uses blue china as a contrast, but this is a much more bustling space and two areas of stronger red – on the screen and the tiles around the fireplace – force the eye to rest for a moment. Note also how, in the second room, the bed has been "tailored" with a matching, pleated valance and upholstered frame to very neat effect, and how the fabric has been used again on the firescreen and in the fireplace beyond.

RED BATHROOMS

*B*athrooms happily lend themselves to riots of colour, pattern, flouncing and ornament. But, unlike other rooms, the whole effect can be subtly reinforced by a suggestion of scent. Subtlety is the key word here – the last thing you want is to reel back before an almost tangible wall of perfume as though a flaçon of "Chanel No.5" had been spilt on the carpet.

If you settle on a rose theme in the bathroom – and pale pinks are ideal in a room which should always feel fresh but warm –

background hints of rosy scent will heighten the luxury of walls swathed in a busy *toile* or windows draped with the most charming of pinky chintzes. Try drops of perfumed oil warmed over a lightbulb, or a 19th-century dish sprigged with roses and filled with the tiny rosebud potpourri sold on the streets of Rome. Then make a vow always to use rose-scented soaps or those, like rose geranium, which complement that perfume. Essential oils in rose and rose geranium can be bought in tiny bottles from the herbalist. Combine them with unscented

Even the water tank is decorated with cabbagey red roses at the Chateau Courance in northern France. Paintings,
porcelain, photograph frames, the hot-water bottle cover – all are strewn with flowers. Almost the only exceptions
are the carpet, the marbled grass-green bath and its surround and the asparagus barrel seat.

Specially faded rose-strewn wallpapers complement traditional bathrooms: (above left) the decision not to conceal the entangled plumbing heightens the old-fashioned effect and (above right), in a room designed for pleasurable pottering, the garlanded bathtub has an almost theatrical air.

The bold, full-bloom red-rose design by Jane Churchill used on all the major surfaces (opposite), including the lavishly "tented" ceiling, is relieved only by a dado and carpet of neutral colouring. The result is an exceptional bathroom which offers a splendidly luxurious retreat from the world beyond.

almond oil to make a perfumed rub or shake a few drops into the bath as it is filling to create a fragrant dip. Then store them in old cut-glass perfume bottles with silver tops, modern ones from such elegant houses as Guerlain and Lancôme or the flowery porcelain dressing-table pots that were made in the 1930s.

If roses seem too clichéd, carnations and their little cousins, the pinks, adapt equally well to the pink floral bathroom, and there are plenty of soaps, potpourri, sprigged papers and fabrics from which to choose. Or why not give an exotic, quirky touch to the bathroom by seeking inspiration in bright 18th-century Indian fabrics, where carnations and their spiky foliage are displayed on plain white backgrounds, or in Persian-influenced tiles? This style can be complemented with flowered Persian pitchers, tiny painted Indian boxes whose tops and sides are strewn with flowers, or marvellously ornate Indian furniture, carved, stamped and inlaid with bands of foliage and flowers. And then complete the effect with the musky scent of carnation.

Because bathrooms are a relatively modern invention, the current craze for period authenticity can be jettisoned without guilt. But, as a rule, bathrooms should be treated like any other room, being given proper furniture and curtains or drapes, pictures or objects on the wall and charming collectibles used to disguise necessities such as toothpaste. The tub – best kept

traditional and white – should also be seen as a piece of furniture. You can plumb it in freestanding and decorate its austere sides. Stencils are perfect on the outsides of metal bathtubs, but be bold. A pastel line of diminutive roses will not do. Strew the outside with them, painted in strong colours. Or box the whole tub in – not with rainforest mahogany but with plastic or hardwood panels covered with wallpaper or fabric, painted with trompe l'oeil or even gilded.

One extremely pretty idea, which I first saw in a house in rural Ireland, is to cut the flowers from a big-patterned floral wallpaper and use the scraps instead of stencils. A long spray of pink roses had actually been used to cover a crack in a mirror but the idea, based on the old craft of decoupage, can be adopted simply for its style. The wallpapers which lend themselves most to this treatment are those with well-defined flowers set on a pale background. Splashily painted papers do not work. The scraps can be stuck on the bath, dado or ceiling moulding or around waste baskets and laundry boxes in varying combinations.

Keep houseplants in your bathroom too: pink cyclamen, hanging fuchsias and even, in summer, scented-leaved pelargoniums or pot geraniums in Italian terracotta. A red bathroom can be part conservatory and part living room – somewhere to put on the rose-coloured glasses and view life with optimism.

The Yellow Anthology

A bright, clear yellow floral print, porcelain, glossy white marble floor tiles and exterior lights directed inward combine to create the brilliant sunshine of Provence in this London basement (opposite). Any other colour would have been alienating amid such brightness. Yellow has brought warmth and comfort to the room.

A 19th-century French print (left) showing several narcissus varieties, none of which are now generally available. Most species of this perennial bulb originated in Europe but others have been found in North Africa and in Asia, where it is still a popular Chinese houseplant. For the key to the fabrics on the previous pages, see page 186.

Only one flower has the distinction of being the symbol of an emperor and that is the golden-yellow chrysanthemum, the personal device of the Emperor of Japan. The Kokako Mikado ennobled the flower in 1797 and put a stylized version of it on his flag. He, and his descendants thereafter, sat on the Chrysanthemum Throne. But long before it was exalted, the chrysanthemum had become so well loved that it was chosen as one of the Seven Flowers of Autumn and awarded its own festival. Versions of it, from those giant incurved balls of petals to the spider chrysanthemums so popular with today's florists, appeared constantly in Japanese paintings and the applied arts. There are chrysanthemums embroidered on kimonos, lacquered on the carefully detailed little nests of medicine or seal boxes called *inro*, inlaid into swords and armour and brightly painted on porcelain designed by the Kakiemon potters.

Like many things Japanese, the flower had in fact made the journey from China some centuries before. The Chinese had cultivated the flower since at least 500BC and were as fond of it as the Japanese, depicting it on bowls and vases, scrolls and embroideries. It was through these objects, imported into Europe, that the West first learned of the chrysanthemum. The actual bloom was not seen until plants arrived in the Netherlands in 1689 (only to die), England in 1764 (never to be heard of again) and France in 1789 (only one plant lasted long enough to flower). It was named after the Greek *khrusos* (gold) and *anthemon* (flower). John Reeves, the Englishman who popularized it in Europe during the 19th century, was an inspector of tea for the British East India Company who lived – and gardened – on China's offshore island of Macao. He planted chrysanthemums in pots, along with other Chinese cultivated species like camellias, peonies and azaleas, let them become well established and then sent them to Europe via the tea clippers.

However, the chrysanthemum never really became popular as a decorative motif in the West, except when Japanese style was all the craze during the Art Nouveau period. This is perhaps because the most attractive of the hundreds of Eastern varieties available, from Japan, China and Korea, were not considered commercially viable by 19th-century plantsmen. It is only now that the more delicate species are finally being grown in the West, largely through the influence of flower arrangers, that we can appreciate its full beauty.

The yellow chrysanthemum may be unique in its association with an emperor, but another yellow flower can claim to have given its name to a dynasty. Broom (or *Genista*) was the symbol of the English Plantagenet kings (*planta-genista*). Legend has it that Fulk, founder of the Plantagenet dynasty (1154-1485), took the plant as his crest after having been scourged with its twigs to atone for the murder of his brother. In the 13th century the sainted Louis IX of France created an order of knighthood called L'Ordre du Genest because of the plant's association with humility. The 100 knights, who formed his bodyguard, wore a gold chain with enamelled links of white fleurs-de-lys and gold broom flowers, from which hung the motto *Deus exaltat humiles*. The Tudor King Henry VIII of England found the plant useful "against surfeits and diseases thereof arising", says the British herbalist John Gerard, writing later in the 16th century. Pickled, it was often used in 16th-century salads and, as its name suggests, its straight, supple twigs were bound together to make brooms. Ignored for centuries, with its spiky green linear stems it is making a comeback in both flower arrangements and fabrics.

Marigolds, originally also called sun-flowers because their yellow daisy-like heads follow the sun around the sky, were once the emblem of jealousy. The association referred back to the Greek myth of Clytie, daughter of King Orchamos of Babylon, deserted by the sun god, who pined away to become the flower which always watches the sun. (The legend is also told of other flowers which follow the sun, notably the heliotrope.) In the 16th century Marguerite de Valois, wife of Henry of Navarre and divorced by him when he became Henry IV of France, chose the flower and the sun as her device, along with the words *Je ne veux suivre que lui seul* ("I wish to follow none but him"). By then, the marigold had lost its bad reputation and come to signify the happiness stored in recollection. And by the end of the 19th century, it was a favourite of the Arts and Crafts Movement.

However, no flower attracted the artists, designers and craftsmen of that movement as much as the true sunflower. It

A 19th-century French print of Chrysanthemum *'Walter Seaman' (above). Vigorous floral cottons mix happily with checks and tartans in a scheme by Designers Guild (opposite), featuring bright yellow rose and primrose fabrics.*

appears, for example, in a 1899 drawing of his studio by the Swedish artist Carl Larsson. Originally from Peru, it later spread to the southern states of North America, where the British explorer and cartographer John White made a detailed drawing of it. It and its cousin, the Jerusalem artichoke, arrived in Europe about 20 years later. The Flemish painter Anthony van Dyck painted himself with such a flower as a symbol of his devotion to Charles I of England. Two centuries later the sunflower had become the symbol of the Aesthetic Movement. It was adopted by the English architect J.J. Stevenson, who popularized the redbrick "Queen Anne" style which quickly crossed the Atlantic, and sunflowers popped up all over redbrick mansions in terracotta panels, on tiles, firescreens and on the faces of clocks, eventually becoming a cliché. *Queen Magazine*, interviewing Stevenson in 1880, wrote, "Cheap buildings are possessed by the idea that red brick, a blue pot and a fat sunflower in the window are all that is needed to be fashionably aesthetic and Queen Anne."

Nature clearly enjoys the colour yellow since so many wildflowers are in its varied shades. Some of the earliest plants cultivated in the West were yellow too, often being wildflowers grown as herbs and used for medicine, to flavour food or to scent musty rooms (whether strewed on the floor or grown in pots). The 16th-century German artist Albrecht Dürer's wonderful watercolour *Das Grosse Rasenstück* meticulously details the simple beauties of a chunk of meadow turf notable for its dandelions. Perhaps Dürer had some message in mind other than the delights of nature because dandelions were considered a symbol of grief and are found in Dutch and German 14th- and 15th-century paintings of Christ's crucifixion.

The coltsfoot, another plant seen today as a pernicious weed, was once considered the perfect remedy for chest problems so Parisian apothecaries would paint its shaggy yellow flowers on their doorposts. In the Highlands of Scotland, its down was used to stuff pillows and, in Bavaria, coltsfoot flowers were thrown into the fire at Easter. In the west of England other yellow flowers were made into garlands at Easter, among them daffodils, jonquils, primroses, polyanthus and catkins, the latter being seen today as a harbinger of spring. But daffodils give rise to many superstitions, such as if the first one you see has its head turned toward you, it means a year's bad luck.

Yellow flowers can be made to suit any interior and should never be dismissed as too pretty for a modern setting or too chintzy for pre-18th century rooms. And because they are probably the most common, both in nature and in cultivation, there is a large number from which to choose. The sunflower (top left) is without doubt one of the boldest of all yellow flowers, instantly able to dominate any space, whereas broom (top right) appeals to subtler instincts and has the advantage of a long flowering season. Wildflowers bunched and thrust into a jug (bottom left) are certain to summon up country style, while stately irises (bottom right) are definitely formal. The brightness of yellow lilies, roses, verbascum, fruit and handsome foliage (opposite) is cleverly magnified by placing an arrangement where it catches the sun. These are all summer arrangements, but for early spring forsythia is useful. It is a flower I could do without, but that is a personal prejudice and in temperate climates its blooms can certainly be forced to arrive before any other spring shrub.

YELLOW ARRANGEMENTS

Some of the earliest blooms of spring are yellow and all of them need intimate treatment because they are extremely small. But, when the huge variety of daffodils, jonquils and narcissi appear, the possibilities increase enormously. The big yellow-trumpeted daffodil begs to be picked in armfuls and pushed into large vases. Yet the more recent varieties with back-tilted petals, curly edges or variegated trumpets reward close examination. So, too, do scented, multiheaded narcissi and jonquils, which can be mixed by shade. Their green spear-like leaves are the only foil they need.

Mimosa never fails to add an exotic touch, bringing the first hint of summer to an arrangement. Unfortunately, two other golden-flowered, extravagantly scented shrubs, Etna and Spanish broom, are very fragile. But in any Mediterranean country home you will see their stark branches on dressers and tables. Preferring a more temperate climate is the simple orangey yellow azalea which grows nearly wild on acid soils. Towns in late spring can content themselves with a lovely pale yellow scented lilac.

By full summer there is a rush of yellow daisy- and buttercup-like flowers – senecio, rudbeckia, hypericum and potentilla. These simple flower forms should be arranged like wildflowers with the feathery leaves of fennel and dill. Achillea, a cultivated milfoil, has stately flat heads and dries very well for winter, and bright chrysanthemums are now available all year to supply the shortage of true winter yellow.

YELLOW LIVING ROOMS

It was the German poet and dramatist Johann Goethe who, in 1780, concluded that blue rooms felt cold whereas yellow rooms were cheering and warming. Twenty years on the notion that yellow was the ideal colour for shady rooms because it gave an impression of warm sunlight had gained currency among decorators all over Europe, and the yellow living room has a firm place in the history of European and American country houses. The 18th-century version tended toward plain or damask silk wallhangings, and modern wallpapers can imitate the all-over floral damasks successfully to create a backdrop of almost plain, washed yellow. In the 19th century, walls and curtains or drapes were decorated with tiny sprigs, bringing a pleasing scale to small, low-ceilinged rooms.

Curiously, however, yellow is not a popular colour in the home today – perhaps because people tend to confine it to dark, shady rooms. But egg-yolk yellow variations of rose-decked chintz and linen are available, as well as all-over foliage and sprig patterns copied from 19th-century fabrics and modern designs featuring detailed flower portraits on a white ground.

Yellow is an ideal colour for cottage homes because it puts up with clutter while harmonizing with the greens outside. The palest primrose, for example, gives a rough plastered living room a warmth that white cannot, and encourages a build-up of quantities of bright fabrics and yellow-daubed pots.

Although theorists believe that yellow reduces the size of a room, it is a colour that readily lends itself to contrasts because it rarely clashes with other colours. But do avoid mixing different tones of yellow. It is important to stick to shades of your chosen tone, whether acid or mellow, when planning a scheme.

Mary Rose Young used many of the exuberant colour combinations she works with in her pottery when she came to decorate the two converted 19th-century cottages which are now her home. Her living room (right) is a lively demonstration of the dictum that Post-Modernist decor puts a ban on clutter. Here bold blocks of primary colours emphasize the few floral decorations. The rose motifs on the hand-painted tiles, the giant hanging cup, the seat of the upright chair, all have folk echoes in Ukrainian embroidery, and there are three-dimensional roses at the ends of the curtain pole and on the spotted and striped punch bowl. Some country cottages open straight through low doorways into the living room, often a dim space with little natural light. Mary Rose Young's hallway (left) has exactly those problems on a smaller scale. Taking the plain terracotta floor and a yellow ceiling as her colour base, she has painted a floral stripe pattern directly onto the walls for instant sunshine.

Yellow is useful in town living rooms to add warmth to high-ceilinged formal surroundings. Here, one scheme (top right) takes the green end of the spectrum for its walls, floors and fabrics, while the second (top and bottom left) uses a much softer, less acid tone and the walls of the third (bottom right) are the dark ochre so popular in Classical Rome. All use creamy yellow through orange floral patterns in the cushions or pillows and upholstery. Richly patterned red or orange rugs add even more warmth to a yellow scheme, but in the

second example (top and bottom left) the effect is counterbalanced by the gray-blue upholstered sofa and upright chairs. Yellow also suits less sophisticated living rooms. At the Second House Museum on Long Island, New York, a diagrammatic all-over patterned fabric creates an understated background for a collection of 19th-century parlour pieces (opposite). The cloth is stretched over battens to conceal the irregular plaster behind – a simple technique, but one that requires forward planning if you intend to hang pictures.

YELLOW DINING ROOMS & KITCHENS

One of the world's most famous sets of crockery is that used by artist Claude Monet at his house in Giverny, France. Ringed with bright Mediterranean blue and acid yellow, he designed it to enhance the country food served in this most Impressionist of houses. Yellow, as he knew, is a colour that encourages the eye to feast on food.

The freshness of bright yellow, blue and white brings the country into any room. For this reason the yellow dining room benefits from some change with the seasons. Case covers for dull dining chairs and the full-length cloth for the table may, in spring, be dotted with pretty flowering bulbs; in summer they could become a riot of nasturtiums, to be replaced by orange-yellow berries in autumn or fall and winter. And the furniture should tend toward the conservatory – creaking wicker chairs with faded floral throws, painted, distressed cupboards or closets and, on the walls, oil paintings of floral still lifes or prints of exotic flowers. This is also the room to benefit from a painted floor.

Unlike treatments for dining rooms in other colours, the yellow dining room translates without alteration into a family kitchen to brighten the saddest city apartment or cheer up any country cottage in the dampest month of the year.

Yellowy floral themes unite the eclectic mixture in a highly individual room (left) with its country furniture, Florentine chair backs, Oriental carpet, colonial floor painting and Japanese-style wallpaper and curtains or drapes. A more traditional room (below) uses a dramatic floral wallpaper and fabric.

YELLOW BEDROOMS & BATHROOMS

*T*here is nothing as uplifting to the spirits as spring. What could be more cheering, therefore, than to wake in the morning to a vibrant yellow bedroom, its walls striped with twining ribbons and flowers, the bedhead and hangings scattered with early spring flowers and, underfoot, a needlepoint carpet of bright yellow posies?

When using yellow shades, it is important to complement the busy patterns of flowery cotton and linen with some solid slabs of a single hue. For example, drape circular bedside tables or nightstands in a pure yellow to pick up the stronger tones in the floral patterns and to patterned curtains or drapes add a border in toning plain fabric.

I am a firm believer in keeping bathroom basics simple – white fixtures, white bathmat and towels, no patterns, no colours. When it comes to creating atmosphere here I prefer not to be restricted by the colours of the towels or tub. But most important of all, bathrooms should be user-friendly. Wallpaper is much more necessary here than in most rooms – anything from tiny sprig patterns covering everything with yellow posies to imposing flourishes of sunflowers or lilies in larger rooms. Fabrics are also excellent in bathrooms so why not try some of those joyful Provençal cottons in yellow?

If the pattern on the walls is not too dramatic, it can be picked up in the curtains or drapes, which should always be very generous in bathrooms. Otherwise, as in the bedroom, a busy pattern on the walls can be given weight by choosing one of the yellows from the design and using it plain in the curtains and carpet. However, when the pattern is small, all-over or monochrome, slabs of colour will not give enough contrast and curtains matching the walls seem to "disappear" so, if the pattern is understated in one element, overstate it in others.

The yellow theme can be continued with floral-scented soaps. Other sources of scent that add a dash of yellow are furry balls of mimosa, dried and used as potpourri, and perfume bottles of citrus scent from the lemon fields of Sicily.

Botanical china plates look good in bathrooms. Pick designs from the narcissus family, or roses and chrysanthemums, and mass them, close together, on one wall. The same can be done with botanical prints, mounted, for extra effect, in yellow. The 19th century produced tole water carriers, their black-painted grounds cheered with yellow daisy borders, and matching trays that look well on the wall. Complete the detailing with a rag rug bursting with yellow daisies and some simple matte gray or white furniture painted with daffodil-yellow posies.

*Bold floral yellows and oranges on floor and ceiling pull
a difficult space together, making this attic a more
welcoming place in which to lay your head.*

The
Blue
Anthology

Ralph Lauren's toning light and dark fabrics take traditional chintz rose patterns and colour them Chinese blue (opposite). The simple ticking on the French formally upholstered daybed and pillows and a plain woollen throw offer a satisfying contrast. On the floor a handsome Chinese carpet, patterned with foliage, is coloured stone and blue.

A 19th-century French print of **Anemone angulosa** *(left). The genus name was once thought to derive from the Greek* **anemos** *(wind) but is now considered to be the Greek version of Naamen, or Adonis, from whose blood the red* **A. coronaria** *is said to have sprung. For the key to the fabrics on the previous pages, see page 187.*

The blue lotus, a type of water-lily, had the same status in ancient Egypt as the rose has in the West today. *Nymphaea caerulea* appears in decor and on objects dating from the Old Kingdom, well before 2600BC; and at Saqqara, near Cairo, there is a carving of a bowl piled high with fruit and lotus flowers, their blue colouring still quite clear. Queen Nefertiti lived in a palace decorated with blue lotus-flower murals, bright blue and turquoise pottery was covered with lotus symbols, and the blue semi-precious stone lapis lazuli was carved to form the elegant bloom. An Egyptian necklace of another blue flower, the cornflower, also still exists. Indeed the Egyptians loved all flowers. They had arrangements in their houses, made wreaths and bouquets for parties, and, a delightful touch, even twined them around the horns of working oxen.

The Chinese were also keen on the lotus flower in decoration. They took it to their hearts along with Buddhism as a symbol of wisdom when the faith travelled east from India along the silk road from the middle of the 1st century BC onward. From India

the lotus-flower symbol also travelled westward, to the Ottoman potters of Isnik, in Turkey, whose white wares were covered with vibrant blue, turquoise and lacquer-red decoration depicting the lotus, carnation, fritillary and tulip in an extraordinary amalgam of Eastern and Western floral motifs.

The rulers of Persia, Turkey and Mughal India were all fascinated by nature and gardening. The first Mughal emperor, Babur, is known to have grown blue flowers such as the hyacinth, larkspur, delphinium, hollyhock and violet. The naturalistic flowers which appear in the paintings, manuscripts, fabrics, clothes, *pietra dura* work and pottery of the period confirm this interest. And there is a charming painting of Babur himself, cross-legged on a comfortable chair, reading in his garden, the whole surrounded by a blue and gilded border decorated with a wavy-leaf design.

Although blue flowers are not particularly common in nature, they are rich in myth and folklore. At least three were described by the Roman poet Ovid as having been created by the gods from dying mortals. Hyacinthus was a beautiful young prince loved by the north and the west winds. Their murderous jealousy was roused when Apollo fell in love with him too, and the story ended tragically. Hyacinthus was killed by a blow from Apollo's discus, directed by the envious winds, and he was immortalized in the lovely scented flower which sprang from his blood. Ajax, a Greek hero of the Trojan War, also came to a flowery end. He threw himself on his sword when he failed to inherit dead Achilles' armour and turned into a larkspur. And the nymph Minthe, fancied by Hades (or Pluto), the god of the underworld, was trodden underfoot by a jealous Persephone, and changed into mint, the toothpaste and chewing-gum herb, by her admirer.

Blue flowers fare equally well in Christ- ian myth and legend. The aquilegia or common columbine is so called because its flowers look like doves in flight and its seven blooms per stem once symbolized the seven gifts of the Holy Ghost. For some reason, this charming fancy did not survive the 16th century, but a glass beaker of columbines stands casually alongside a maiolica vase of tall lilies and irises in the stable in Hugo van der Goes' 15th- century painting *The Adoration of the Shepherds*, now in the Uffizi Gallery in Florence. Irises were, along with lilies, a symbol of the Virgin Mary, largely, it seems, because northern Europe confused the two flowers. So this little floral tableau has columbines for the presence of the Holy Ghost and lilies and irises for the virgin. But the painting's floral symbolism does not end there. Scattered on the stable floor are deep purple violets; the flower that represents both Christian humility and the Christ child, they are frequently to be found in depictions of the Adoration.

The violet has been a favourite in both East and West for centuries. The Persians and the Romans drank violet wine and in the Middle Ages the best poet in French troubador contests was awarded a golden token shaped like a violet. It is also one of the few flowers that are still candied today; its pretty purple petals appear notably on chocolate creams.

Another legendary favourite all over the Mediterranean is the herb rosemary, from the Latin *ros-marinus* ("dew of the sea"). Although its flowers are often bright blue or purple, the Spaniards say that rosemary was white until the Virgin threw her blue robe over the plant during the flight into Egypt; for them, it has power against the evil eye. In the 14th century, Jeanne de

A 19th-century French print of Platycodon grandiflorus *(above). Colefax and Fowler create a monochromatic scheme (opposite), using "Plumbago Bouquet" chintz on the upholstery and curtains or drapes and "Blue Pheasant Eye" on the walls.*

Valois, the Countess of Hainault, mother of Queen Philippa of England, claimed that it made all who use it cheerful: "The leves layde under the heade whanne a man slepes, it doth away evell spirites and suffereth not to dreeme fowle dremes he to be afeade." She went on to say that rosemary never grows higher than the height of Christ and that once a plant grows that tall it will only increase in breadth. Of course, the mad Ophelia offers rosemary "for remembrance" in Shakespeare's *Hamlet*, a reference to the custom, in Tudor times, of throwing sprigs of the herb onto the graves of loved ones. It was also carried at funerals, burned in sick rooms, used to ward off black magic and as a strewing herb in homes and churches. The superstition that rosemary drives out devils – and the plague – has persisted for centuries and, of course, blue has always been thought of as a lucky colour. Brides must traditionally wear something blue. But other blue flowers may be less welcome. For example, hydrangeas must not be planted too close to the house if you want your daughter to marry, and the tiny blue speedwell must never be picked or the birds will peck your eyes out. How these ill omens would fare if you were protected with rosemary, or that other lucky blue plant, vervain, is hard to guess. But Pliny, writing about Gaul in Roman times, said that vervain was carried by hostages for luck, used to purify houses and, if rubbed on the body, would grant your wishes. Blue-flowered thyme is more a favourite with fairies, they say, as is the foxglove, whose little bells are traditionally called fairies' havens.

Borage is another intensely blue flower much loved by herbalists. The traditional saying "I, borage, always bring courage" was originally Greek but, the story goes, it reached northern Europe via the Roman occupation. A 16th- century herbalist believed that a conserve of the flower was "especially good against melancholie; it maketh one merie" – and so did Pliny the Elder, who called the plant *euphrosynum* because it made men joyful. Along with the blue-flowered bugloss (otherwise known as anchusa or alkanet), the violet and the rose, it was one of four "cordial" flowers used to cheer the heart. In the past – though sadly not for several centuries – borage flowers were a favourite with embroiderers. However, borage is still thrown into summery glasses of Pimms, both for its flavour and its colour. Perhaps a sprig of thyme should be added too – thyme soup was once prescribed as a cure for shyness.

Almost all true blue arrangements are essentially passive in mood with the notable exceptions of tiny gentians, which look best alone in a plain glass globe, and certain varieties of delphinium. Helped by small triangular vases wired behind the main arrangement, delphiniums can be made taller still – even a small room with one empty corner can cope with such grandeur. For arrangements which dominate you must turn to the redder end of the blue spectrum as it swings from purple toward mauve: (top left) a casual assembly of purple delphiniums, steel-blue echinops and gray-blue eucalyptus foliage; (top right) separate vases of tall larkspur, brodiaea and white sweet peas in a monochrome scheme; (bottom left) spikes of veronica and darker blooms add a velvety glow to creamy cow parsley, echoing the wallpaper beyond; (bottom right) a cloud of wildflowers for a chest set against partition planking, and (opposite) dried flowers for any season – clumps of lavender, statice and hydrangea among seedheads of barley and poppy.

BLUE ARRANGEMENTS

*T*he blue spectrum contains some of the largest and smallest blooms around. The clear blue of delphiniums is frequently used for midsummer arrangements and the tall flower spikes, covered with blooms, are ideal for grand, formal effects. Two other tall, showy blue flowers are the South African lily, the agapanthus, and the garden allium, a relative of wild garlic, which produces perfect pom-pom heads that make wonderful punctuation points in an arrangement. Spiky thistle and sea-holly flowers will also ensure that a bouquet has strength as well as prettiness. At the other end of the scale are the intimate little midnight-blue and purple violets. These should be massed together – bunches stuffed into small glass vases, tall champagne flutes and silver beakers – and then grouped together on a tabletop. Pansies, grape hyacinths and squills have the same shy charm.

The blue herbs are useful too. Borage's bright flowers contrast with its hairy leaves, and rosemary and lavender flowers come in dainty spikes, whereas those of the sage plant are bolder.

There are also quite a few blue-tinged leaves around. Some hostas have large, striking bluish leaves, and rue, a medicinal herb, has raggedly cut foliage. Eucalyptus is useful because of the interesting contrast of its smoky blue leaves with its pinkish stems, and also because it lasts well in water. Finally, in winter there are blue berries – mahonia is good, so too is berberis.

BLUE LIVING ROOMS

*B*lue is the colour of distance – the longest view finally recedes into pale lilac and empty, cloudless skies, deep lakes and oceans are all blue. Although it is a cold, sometimes even frightening colour, blue is also at its strongest in heat. In Sweden, in that cool, white northern light, living rooms are painted the blue-gray of mist in winter, but in the Greek islands or in New Mexico or California strong ultramarines and cobalts decorate shutters and furniture alike. Too strong a blue will seem garish under a weak sun, yet the same tone in Italy or Spain will temper the heat and give relief from the glare outside.

Blues also divide into two categories. At one end of the spectrum are the reddish blues – from purple and mauve through ultramarine to sky-blue. At the other are the green-blues, more assertive colours, from the palest turquoise, the colour found in the early 19th-century Neoclassical rooms of French society hostesses such as Madame de Récamier, to deep indigo and Prussian blue, the near-black tones dyed into Indonesian flowered batiks and Spanish moreens and damasks.

The red-blues are constantly found in nature and easily adapt to the shabby chic of the English country house or cottage living room. Faded chintzes, once royal blue and now hyacinth, combine with soft Wilton carpets or needlepoint rugs. Sofas covered in flowery linens of shadowed grape and pale fuchsia loll beside fireplaces surmounted by mirrors and pretty flower-painted spill-holders. These are the rooms for charming watercolours painted by 18th-century ladies who could catch the meaning at the heart of an auricula, where powder-blue ribbons are used to join up arrangements of little gold-framed miniatures and where wallpapers are festooned with hydrangea-blue flowers set against broad leaves. Here pretty blue and white fabrics can disguise lowly round tables. Let them fall in generous folds to the floor and crowd the tabletops with Chinese blue-flowered porcelain, the clutter of silver photograph frames, blue-flowered pomanders filled with scented potpourri and those wooden marbled blue and silver spheres still created in Rome. All this may seem summery, but in winter blue rooms become cosy with log fires and bunches of blue-gray berries.

Salons in the sun are more formal and it is the blue which leans to the green end of the spectrum that provides the base for such rooms. That indeterminate pale colour, in one light blue, in another green or turquoise, has been used everywhere for the most precious silks and satins, as a background in Aubusson carpets and for painted ceilings. The pale flowers of iris and columbine, the leaves of olive, lavender and sage have been the inspiration for this mysterious colour, which has been painted on walls since ancient Egypt and Minoan Crete.

Blue can be made to say many things in the floral living room. Its flowers are used to decorate the formal Rococo ceilings of the grandest princely palazzo or the simply daubed peasant armoire in a French provincial farmhouse. Quite simply, for me it is the colour I can never have too much of.

A fine collection of Chinese blue and white jars and vases densely patterned with flowers and foliage were the starting point for this charming, light French living room (opposite), decorated by Ralph Lauren. The warm tones of antique, long-polished wood, the touches of red on the handsome clock and porcelain bowl filled with scented potpourri, and the creamy whites of the wool throw, the rug and the flowers prevent the scheme from tipping over into coldness. I have also seen a kind of warmth brought to a cool blue interior with those extraordinary jewelled trees made of precious crystal, jade and lapis lazuli which come from China. They brought nature indoors in the most costly manner and, stood cleverly on a mantelpiece against a faded, foxed old mirror, the gem flowers seemed to bloom for a second time. Vases of Wedgwood blue with white bas-reliefs of Classical scenes could be the starting point for a gray-blue floral scheme.

A detail of a room, in fact a bedroom, planned around a Chinese theme (left) – Chinoiserie as explored in antique Delft ware (for other views of this room see pages 69 and 123). The enviable selection of pieces grouped together here would be equally at home in the living room. Even the cow is flower-decked. Blue Delft tiles, each painted with a bouquet or some exotic animal, have traditionally covered country fireplaces. If you are lucky enough to have or acquire one, play it to the hilt by making the mantelshelf busy with blue and white Chinese vases, dishes, flower bricks and incense holders. The Portuguese also loved blue and white tiles – indeed, Portuguese tiles are still known as azulejos – and they perfected the art of huge tiled pictures. Blue florals can work particularly well in the casual garden room – a place of flowers and sunlight with blinds or shades to shield its glass roof – and this is probably because many blues look good alongside the green spectrum.

BLUE DINING ROOMS & KITCHENS

Collectors of antique porcelain used to consider blue and white pieces beneath their notice. Today, there is less on the market, but even so there is no shortage. English and Continental 18th-century manufacturers all took their lead from the Chinese originals which first arrived in Europe in the 17th century.

The early 19th-century English dining room in a fashionable house was therefore probably designed to suit blue and white floral china, its cool shades emphasized by table silver, a floral Persian carpet with a dark blue background and a blue damask silk or paper on the walls. It is equally likely that the fine shield-back Hepplewhite chairs or the Chinese Chippendale carvers (themselves the product of the craze for Chinoiserie) were upholstered in pale blue silk damask – ample proof that their owner was unconcerned with the business of cleaning them.

In the rest of Europe, from France to Sweden, Poland to Portugal, and in the United States, blue was also the predominant colour in the dining rooms of the period. Swedish tiled stoves, once again being manufactured, were patterned in blue and fireplaces in Holland were edged with Delft tiles of flowers or windmilled landscapes.

Blue remained a favourite throughout the 19th century. The same flowery, spriggy patterns went down the social scale to adorn the thicker white ware made in England's Staffordshire potteries and throughout France, where it was called *faïence* (a corruption of Faenza, the Italian town renowned for its 15th- and 16th-century blue-patterned chargers, urns and apothecary's jars). Staffordshire plates are still available in abundance, although now the carvers are more likely to hang on the wall, their edges bordered with blue roses, their middles filled with formal bouquets of exotic blooms. And factories from Copenhagen to Spode still make the same blue-transfer services.

These wares are as much at home in the family kitchen as the formal dining room, and fabrics and wallpapers influenced by Chinese porcelain add to their charm. For example, the Portuguese weave reversible blue and white floral bedspreads that are the ideal size to cover a farmhouse table. French napkins, embroidered in white on blue, or little Eastern European ones, cross-stitched in a semblance of the willow pattern, will continue the theme. Tiles are also at home here. The blue and white Mediterranean versions currently imported throughout the West make pretty splashbacks to sinks, edges around working surfaces or even serve as the surfaces themselves.

All detail in this living cum dining room à deux has been countrified. The ornate upholstered furniture, decked with Waverly's "Sweet Violets", is in 19th-century style but the wicker and tiled floor change pace, the latter deliberately evoking a Dutch interior.

BLUE BEDROOMS

J like blue in bedrooms. The darker shades have an affinity with night-time and, because blue recedes, it is restful and conducive to sleep. Also, although true blue is perhaps the colour with the fewest flowers, it is nonetheless one which designers for years have used for some of their best work.

Indigo, one of the most commonly used early vegetable dyes, was not an easy colour to control yet the French made valiant attempts with the *toiles* produced at Jouy, Nîmes and Mulhouse. Much rarer than the madder-pink fabrics, enough blue prints survive to make us long for more. Luckily, modern fabric/wallpaper specialists like Burger and Zuber in France, Marvic and Baker in England and Brunschwig in the United States all try hard to recapture their sophisticated charm.

French country cottons – tickings and other, later *toiles* – were traditionally used in large quantities as bedhangings and quilts, and it would be a charming idea to re-create one of these upholstered four-posters. Originally, the patterned fabric was used only on the exterior hangings, with either a plain blue or unobtrusive sprig facing inward. Hangings were hand stitched in diamonds about 2 inches (5cm) across but today a sewing machine does the job just as well. Curtains or drapes in this French country bedroom would be kept simple. Outer ones – for decoration – might be made of the same fabric as the bed. Inner lace or simple cotton voile would keep out the sun while wooden louvred shutters made the room airy but dark at night.

A pretty blue wallpaper influenced equally by toile de Jouy *and Chinoiserie (above) makes an ideal background for a collection of modern Chinese portraits and flower paintings. The Indian chair, inlaid with mother-of-pearl daisies, takes up the Oriental theme and the fan motifs carved on the antique chest of drawers are an added refinement. Cross-cultural mixing is also apparent in a blue bedroom at the Chateau de Morsan in France (right), designed by the owner, an expert in 17th- and 18th-century European history. Hand-painted motifs derived from Delft vases decorate the walls and Indian-inspired blue and white fabric decks the romantic canopied bed and curtains or drapes. In complete contrast is the serene bedroom (overleaf), designed by the head of Colefax and Fowler for a house in the hills behind Nice (see also page 115). The diagrammatic sprigs used on the walls and on the carpet, Colefax and Fowler's "Tatton Park", provide a sympathetic background for the beautiful chintz pattern. Note also the subtle changes of pattern and texture – on the rugs (even in the pet basket), the luggage stand and the winged chair.*

BLUE BATHROOMS

*J*n the floral home, the blue-decorated bathroom will always have a relaxed country air, whether it is a large first-floor room in a country house, the bath freestanding as though it were a piece of furniture, or a windowless space tucked into a passageway in a city apartment. Because blue has such an easy-going affinity with white – and white linen, basin, bathtub and so on are very evident in the best bathrooms – the atmosphere will naturally be lighthearted.

Start with the pervasive scent of bluebell, in bath oil and essence, in eau de toilette, soap and shampoo, all in old-fashioned glass bottles and wooden tubs, and let the blue bathroom be a place which soothes the senses. Take quantities of Chinese blue and white floral dishes and fill them with blue bathsalts and little guest soaps, pressed into the shape of flowers or hearts. And contrast the cool white linen hand-towels with great cornflower-blue bathsheets, fluffy navy bathmats and flannels ranging from ice-blue to marine – my strictly puritanical taste weakens where blue is concerned.

The bathroom is the place for extravagant wallpaper. For a start, it generally does not need too many rolls (especially if a useful dado is fitted) and so beautiful and complex patterns come within the reach of most pockets. And because it needs little paper, bold designs are not *de trop*. Besides, lying in the suds encourages contemplation of the complexities and colours around you. One paper which would look delightful in a blue floral bathroom is Baker's charmer of blue cow parsley, vine leaves and grapes abuzz with sparrows. Manuel Canovas' big blue flowers on creamy white backgrounds are excellent here too (and anywhere else, it must be said), as are John Stefanides' stylized Mediterranean-blue florals. French all-over florals

nearly always come in blue colourways and have an 18th-century pastoral charm well worth cultivating. These can be teamed with plain floating curtains or drapes, several shades paler or darker. Or let the walls be plain and the curtains delightfully flowery. The latter naturally works best when there are either plenty of windows or great expanses of fabric. Large patterns are not at their best when skimped.

The posy papers of 19th-century cottage rooms exert an equal charm. Colefax and Fowler's classic and ageless "Berkeley Sprig" lifts the dullest bathroom, as do flowery patterns by such firms as Laura Ashley and, from Provence, in France, Souleiado. But use them with a controlled hand. Try wallpaper contrasted with plain blue fabrics, ticking or gingham, or make plain blue walls the background to generous floral curtains or drapes and use complementary fabrics for cushions or pillows piled on white country wicker chairs.

If the bathroom is large enough or simply never steams up, I like the idea of furnishing it as a pretty country living room. Along with the chintz and cotton should be flowery beadwork cushions or pillows, bunches of bright blue cornflowers stuffed into those Staffordshire jugs printed with swags of hops, vines and barley (clearly originally designed for ale) and standing on tables covered in frothy white lace. Or the room can be given the air of a Mediterranean outdoor living room, with several painted wooden chairs, great blue-patterned chargers full of dried lavender or bleached shells, and chestnut baskets, filled with blue dried flowers, poised on plain blue-painted armoires.

Then, after a dip in the hyacinth- or lavender-scented bath, a rub-down with aromatic blue bath oil and a towelling from a huge navy bathsheet, wrap up in a flower-embroidered silk dressing gown and let the cares of the day fall away.

The finest blue-flowered voile from Laura Ashley allows most of the available light to flood into this attic bathroom (right) and a smaller, paler flower-patterned paper helps control the angled ceiling. Add the colour-washed wood of the bathtub surround and floorboards and the unusual cord-and-metal chair and the resulting effect is a lighthearted mood that is echoed by the carefree bunches of flowers. Note the pretty blue floral border around the bathtub and the three old flowery plates placed where their detail can be enjoyed at leisure. Draped with a floor-length tablecloth as here, a useful little circular table can be easily and inexpensively achieved by securing a circle of chipboard to any junk stool unfit for view.

Based on a traditional chintz motif, this unusual stylized floral paper sets sharply delineated pale blue flowers and leaves with more than a hint of India on a delicate tracery of diagrammatic foliage. It has a period feel well suited to this deliberately old-fashioned room, and the resulting all-over pattern creates a sympathetic, understated background for a disparate group of pictures which is unified only by a common country theme – the business of hunting. The pretty little faux *bamboo mirror hung above the basin or sink is a happy find because it contrives a link both with the black-framed pictures and the wallpaper. The carpet, the rug, the toothmug and even the marbled bathtub are other variations on the blue theme.*

The Green Anthology

Varying leaf shape, colour and texture provide all-year pleasure in a dining room set in a glass extension (opposite), planted with bamboo, ficus, schefflera and miniature orange trees. The theme is echoed by the leafy tablecloth, and the earthy tones of the terracotta tiles and chair covers also bridge the gap between indoors and outdoors.

A 19th-century French print of the a dwarf form from Japan now renamed **Arundinaria**. Bamboo was variegated **Bambusa fortunei** (left), a favourite subject of the Chinese calligraphers, who strove to reach into the spirit of the plant before putting brush to scroll. For the key to fabrics on the previous pages, see page 187.

*F*ew flowers are coloured green – nicotiana, alchemilla and the hellebores spring to mind, as well as the tiny sprays produced by mosses, lichens and ferns – but green foliage has been an important influence on the floral home and its decor. The only major colour which is not a primary (although it feels as if it should be), its associations are often contradictory. On the one hand, green is the soothing shade of woodlands and grassy meadows, the colour which suggests fresh air and relaxation. And so it can in the home if you choose the right tone. On the other hand, it is the colour associated with jealousy, one which actors used to believe it was bad luck to wear and one which, painted to waist-height in unappealing glossy tones, reminds me of uncaring, run-down institutional buildings. The same contradictions exist in mythology as green leaves can have both negative and positive values.

In the ancient Middle Eastern civilizations of Mesopotamia and Assyria, more than 1,000 years BC, trees were considered holy and there are reliefs of king and genies holding sacred pine cones. There is even, dating from around 2000BC, an Assyrian seal showing a scene not unlike the fall of Adam and Eve, complete with serpent and central tree. Jehovah, god of the Israelites, disapproved of this worship; the Old Testament says the Lord was angered by the holding of ceremonies "under every green tree". Yet such reverence was not surprising in the desert, and the holiest trees were the palm, the pomegranate and the pine.

The garlands of bay leaves twisted around the heads of Greek heroes were an obvious symbol of conquest. Somewhat later, the Greeks declared the oak sacred to Zeus, the king of the gods, and garlands of oak are still a common theme in fabric and architectural decoration. As long as 4,000 years ago, the Minoan court on Crete was decorating its walls with sprays of olives, and the gray-green spiky leaves of the olive were later sacred to Athene, the Greek goddess of wisdom. In the Bible the olive branch was a symbol of peace or reconciliation because it was carried by the dove when it returned to Noah's ark after the waters had receded, following the Great Flood.

Another leaf often used in decoration by the ancients was the ivy. Ascribed to Bacchus, it was the sign of immortality, not least because of its persistence. (The Persians planted cypress trees around their houses to symbolize life after death.) Bacchus also took the vine and grape as his symbols, for obvious reasons, and you can be almost certain that any room with vine-leaf plasterwork or a vine-decorated fireplace was intended as a dining room. The vine was also a symbol of the Early Christian Church and it is often found on sarcophagi in the catacombs of Rome. Its downside is that it also represents the sad season of autumn or fall – and gluttony. To the Victorians, because of its clinging tendrils, the vine was a symbol of fidelity but so also were the ivy and (much less understandably) veronica, whereas the ancients preferred to place the myrtle in that role.

The green plant best loved by the Chinese is the bamboo. Along with the pine and prunus, it was one of the Three Friends of Winter, and, with the epidendrum (a kind of orchid), one of the Four Noble Plants. Its drooping leaves denoted modesty but, more to the point, any serious calligrapher would spend years studying its shifting form. It naturally appears a great deal in Chinese art and, later, was also a major feature of Japanese painting and wood-block printing.

In ancient Egypt it was the papyrus, lotus and palm tree which were revered for their looks and usefulness and which were translated from the field and garden into the decor of the house. In his book *The Grammar of the Lotus*, published in 1891, the American art historian W.H.

A 19th-century French print of a fern (above), titled Calamus linderi. *Foliage motifs on a rich brocade set against warm, deep chestnut panelling (opposite) demonstrate how relatively small touches of green can refresh even the darkest period interior.*

Goodyear suggests that it was the form of the lotus leaf, used by the Egyptians to decorate the capitals of their temple columns, which later became the acanthus and palmette of classical Greek architecture, such as are found in the Erechtheion, built c. 420-406BC beside the Parthenon in Athens. It is certain that the ancient Egyptians were extremely fond of the lotus – the blue-flowered version was sacred to Horus, the falcon or falcon-headed god, and the symbol of regeneration – but the papyrus with its green fluffy flowers was even more popular, being as common in Egyptian decor as the rose is in the West today. For example, it appears on a mural in the temple of Karnak and at the palace of Akhenaton at Tell-el-Amarna.

Most of the gardens of the ancient world tended to be green – perhaps because plants such as figs, palms, olives and vines provided food as well as shelter and shade and because, in the fierce climate, they were more adaptable than flowering plants. It is now known that the Egyptians were fervent gardeners and imported cedar and fruit trees, vines and herbs. They grew figs, dates, olives and vines, and all appeared in their home and tomb decoration. At Assyrian Nineveh, in Ashurbanipal's garden, there were trees and vines, tame birds sang and harpists entertained at outdoor parties. The stone floors of the palace also celebrated nature with mosaics of rosettes, palmettes and lotus flowers. Apples, grapes, pomegranates, olives, figs and herbs appeared as swags and garlands on Greek pottery. And, in the East, the Persian conquests of Alexander the Great, king of Macedon, extended to the River Indus, which may be the reason why Indian cotton chintzes often carried acanthus borders.

Roman gardens were not much different. Plane trees, ivy, box or boxwood, laurel bushes and rosemary have all been reported – and we have Pliny the Elder's revealing account of the garden he built in what is now Tuscany in the 1st century AD. We know that he clipped his boxwood trees into animal shapes and grew them to surround a grass lawn. Planes and cypresses, their trunks covered with ivy, were planted for shade. There were architectural features, such as shady arbours and obelisks, mingled with fruit trees. Fountains and rills provided cool, splashing water. Pliny also created an outdoor dining space at one end of his house's portico. From it, the green formal garden, succeeded by carefully manicured meadows, was visible down a long slope. In Roman villas and townhouses the same plants appeared as decoration in both mosaics and carvings, and the swagged and garlanded plants that often appear on Greek domestic pottery feature here too.

The influence of Rome spread far and, by the time that the Roman Empire fell, these symbols had become an integral part of Western civilization. The shafts of Anglo-Saxon crosses decorated with vines, palmettes and acanthus have been unearthed in England. And carving at Chartres cathedral in northern France revels in ivy, holly and the more temperate hawthorn. It was the reverence that Mediterranean countries had for the olive, fig, lotus and palm that led directly to the Classical decoration on the columns of Andrea Palladio's 16th-century villas near Vicenza in northern Italy and thence, ultimately, to that on the 18th-century townhouses of London and New Orleans.

GREEN ARRANGEMENTS

*A*n arrangement that uses only the green palette is not as difficult to produce as it might seem. True, there are very few green flowers around but that still leaves you with foliage, stems, buds and even fruit and vegetables. Just consider the wonderful variety that this offers.

There are the leaves that look like sculpture – water-lily pads, crinkled lotus leaves, heavily veined ornamental thistles and the spikes of acanthus – and many that are indispensible to the arranger, such as the swordlike iris and yucca, the striped and variegated shields of hostas, and the translucent newly opened buds of lime and beech. And there are the more delicate trailers and fillers: vine and hop tendrils, and the Chinese calligraphy of bamboo, orchid and wisteria.

Take your inspiration from the planting schemes of those who strive to create all-green gardens. For example, look at the way varying leaf forms are emphasized by contrast with their opposites. Try spears with circles, crinkles with satiny, downy types, or massed tiny leaves with huge, unfolding ones. Experiment by mixing green stems with smooth bark, such as cornus, or with flaking bark, such as maple, to build the skeleton

of your arrangement. Then fill the spaces in between with fluffy indeterminate leaves, such as asparagus fern, to provide a "backdrop" for the action.

Give yourself an amusing challenge by planning an arrangement using just one genus. For example, try the hostas, whose leaves are heavily veined, crisped and curved, turning back on themselves or rolling inward, and whose flowerheads, before they open, add that extra dimension of spikiness. Arrangements of vines, grasses, bamboos, pelargoniums (or pot geraniums) or herbs would all offer the same enjoyment, although with vines you would probably need to use more than one genus.

Or what about trying to reverse expectations so that all the flowers are green and all the leaves are definitely not? Take such green flowers as nicotiana, hellebore, greeny white tulips or snowdrops, alchemilla or the buds of unopened bluebells, gladioli or iris, and team them with the furry gray leaves of lamb's lugs and thistle, the yellow varieties of shrubs like philadelphus, yew or holly, the blues of eucalyptus and rue, and the white sports of variegated ivies and grasses to create a negative image. Green flower arrangements are perverse, unusual and very striking. Make the most of them.

Green flowers, or more usually foliage, bring an unmatched vitality to any room and they can brighten a dark corner or cool hectic tones as the occasion demands. A huge Mason's ironstone footbath filled with bright leaves and honesty heads (opposite) lightens the clutter of a tiny entrance hall. A more sophisticated hallway (below left) demands a formal approach and gets it with a stalk of greeny orchids and two

wonderfully dramatic leaves, which strike an exotic mood to complement the marble-topped console table, the metal urns filled with dried lavender, the file of prints and the red-blue decor. A desktop arrangement works best when it invites contemplation, and a bunch of limey alchemilla, coppery proteus and white-variegated euphorbia (below right), thrust into a simple pot, offer a startling variety of greens.

GREEN LIVING ROOMS

*B*ecause green is the colour that we associate with living things, it is easy to live with. And this is especially true of the bright tones that remind us of young shoots and grasses. Some decorators believe that the farther you are from the country, the more necessary its colours are in the home. A country cottage can exist happily with the browns and reds of earth and bricks, but when bricks, stone and lurid posters make up the colours out-of-doors, it is good sense to bring the shades of nature indoors.

The English country style which has swept the world – and nowhere more than in urban jungles like New York – depends for its uniqueness on natural forms. I defy anyone to create a typical English living room without using a single green leaf. Of course, there will be the usual chintzy flowers, but backing them up will be the sparer forms of leaves. Where once every country house had gardeners and glasshouses galore to supply their needs, today the mistress of the house must contrive to create great vases and bowls full of cut branches. But plant material makes its own demands because the designs on fabrics, papers, carpets and paintings must bear some resemblance to the real thing arranged in the vases nearby.

The French have always enjoyed using green indoors and their passion for it heavily influenced the countries of northern Europe throughout the 18th century. But, whereas the walls of their living rooms were rarely patterned, except for wall-paintings or the self-coloured foliage of damask, the French allowed themselves some latitude with large, leafy designs on painted armchairs and, of course, Aubusson carpets broke with the traditions of Oriental design, which employed generally unspecific small flowers, to establish a different formality, using foliage. Borders created from the patterns of Classical wreaths – of bay, oak and olive – contained other plants regimented in a style not unlike the plain green parterres of 17th- and 18th-century French garden design.

From France also came the beautiful monochrome *toile*-type patterns which evolved from the original Arcadian and patriotic scenes to include beautifully detailed plants, leaves and flowers in razor-sharp copperplate designs. Use them in the green living room for covers, cushions or pillows, or for upholstering upright chairs. Use them for the walls of smaller rooms to suggest the anteroom, high yet square, that appears before the *grand salon* in a French chateau. And use them in those awkwardly shaped rooms which result when a grand house of high-ceilinged rooms is split into apartments, turning that lack of proportion into a deliberate design statement.

Most people, if their happiness depended upon it, could foreswear the primary colours. But all of us who love our surroundings would be miserable without a touch of green.

Sanderson's leafy "Loxley" fabric and wallpaper (opposite) has a period feel matched by the prints above the sofa. Note the hint of green in the piping on the glazed cotton cushions or pillows.

At the lighter side of a semi-circular room (see overleaf and page 155), green leaf motifs are explored on pottery and fabric. The pale, mint-coloured walls and neutral sofa pull the scheme into focus.

GREEN DINING ROOMS & KITCHENS

In 19th-century England, Wedgwood, the Staffordshire pottery, created a series of plates moulded in the shape of handfuls of vine or strawberry leaves with crinkled edges. All were coloured a strong, deep green, and the thick, glutinous glaze gathered in the folds and angles of the impressed leaves. These plates have been in regular production ever since and there is good reason for their popularity. Take a handful of cheese straws, a couple of dozen black olives, a tomato salad garnished with basil leaves or a punnet full of strawberries and lay them out on these green dishes and the food immediately looks more colourful, more luscious and more appetizing. Green leaves and good food are instantly complementary. And so it naturally follows that green-leaved dining rooms make good sense.

Of course, the leaves connected with food have long been used in the architecture of the dining room. Neoclassical houses frequently have plasterwork featuring twined vine leaves and heavy grapes, as well as fire surrounds decorated with the same motifs. Ivy, olive and fig leaves are also common, whereas bay leaves make fine garlands on wallpapers and carpets (and are put in beef stews for their flavour).

Until the 18th century dining rooms were rare. A folding table was usually opened up and prepared in the drawing room or secondary reception room in front of the fire or a window, depending on the season. But when the fashion for a separate room emerged around the end of the century, dining rooms immediately took on the role of paterfamilias in the family of rooms (the drawing room, always much lighter and prettier, reflecting the mistress's taste). Ranks of family portraits hung here and, to show up their glinting gold frames, the walls were generally lined with dark silk damasks or papers imitating their formal, floral patterns. Purples, blues and reds were used – but the favourite was a sombre green. Indeed, throughout much of the 18th century green was the most fashionable of all colours, despite (or perhaps, because of) the fact that its chemical mix made it far more expensive than any other. Late in the century curtains or drapes also tended toward the ponderous. Great swags of wool or silk, again damask-patterned and held by gilded tie-backs, were common, their weighted ends blocking out light and sound alike.

Today, there are signs that the era of the dining room is drawing to a close. Crowded urban spaces rarely allow for a room to be kept apart simply for eating. Modern families now eat wherever suits them best. The family kitchen has already arrived; the unfolding table in the living room is again quite common; and a newer fashion, the garden room, conservatory or sun space, seems set to take advantage of hot summers. The garden room is especially at home with the green spectrum – but try an altogether brighter, more cheerful colour. For example, take the delightful papers and fabrics which place trellises of leaves on a plain white ground – ivy, bamboo, vine or hop – or the intricacies of fern leaves used almost as a bouquet and put them together with real plants in a room facing out onto a garden or tree-filled square. Add that Wedgwood leafy pottery, along with heavy green glasses from Portugal, and you have a room for long Sunday lunches made drowsy by beakers full of Pimms with borage and mint leaves, julep or planters' punch. Such a room works well at night too, especially if the garden beyond can be highlighted with outdoor lights that throw special plants into focus and create mysterious shadowy depths.

Green lends itself to themed designs. Obvious are the most popular leaves in decor: the bamboo, ivy and vine. All are available in wallpapers, fabrics, carpets, ceramics, paintings and metalware. The real plants can be grown alongside and for special celebrations their leaves arranged on – or, in the case of poisonous ivy, wreathed around – plates. For example, vine leaves look charming under a pat of butter or slipped under a heap of delicate green grapes. I have also seen acid green Granny Smith apples piled high in a formal pyramid in a black cast-iron urn. They looked wonderfully Neoclassical.

So far I have talked only about urban rooms, but green is just as happy in the country, although I am one of those who believe that it is less necessary to the spirit when there are green fields all around to rest the eye. Consider using those heavy French country-style pottery plates made in Vallauris, their shade lighter than the Wedgwood ones but the glaze even more glutinous. Or white Limoges pottery, its sides painted with sprigs of leaves. It is common in France to decorate huge country dressers with ranks of green leafy plates – some resembling artichokes, others sunflowers. Piled high behind great pottery containers for oil, wine and salt, they give a family kitchen all the ornament and character it needs.

Green is clearly an extremely adaptable colour. Frequently a foil for bright flowers, it can create the background for any colour scheme and this is nowhere more useful than in the dining room, where the main interest should ultimately be in the food itself. Just as those Wedgwood and Vallauris plates will pep up the tomatoes and strawberries arranged on them, so a leafy green dining room is always certain to provide a restful setting for the exciting business of eating.

Foliage forms dominate the decoration of this handsome American Empire dining room in a grand New York mansion. The wallpaper, called "Morning Glory", is a modern copy by Scalamandre of an original dating from the 1770s. In skilled hands the panel and frieze effects could be emulated with stencilling.

New techniques of preservation plus a romantic love of the Gothick meant that ferns became the rage in the 19th century. Species from all over the world were collected by plant hunters and carefully arranged in special grottoes and ferneries. At the same time botanists began to describe and identify the new introductions and this led to the production of delicate prints of the lacy fronds. Books of 19th-century illustrations are now highly sought after for their decorative value. This group of pressed ferns (right) is over 100 years old and is appropriately displayed, without mounts, in the plainest possible gold frames. You can press your own ferns by placing them between several sheets of newspaper under a rug that gets little traffic.

This 19th-century bedroom (opposite) at the Second House Museum on Long Island, New York, is decorated with a sequence of coordinating paper, border and fabric by Waverly. Both the quilt and the attic walls are covered in a stylized trellis pattern, "Ashley"; made of massed ivy leaves, it works well on the angled surfaces. The green and white border pattern around the dado, called "Melanie", is of lilies of the valley. The room's designer has been clever enough to know when to stop – matching curtains would have been too overwhelming whereas plain white shutters enhance the scheme. The flower arrangement is also restricted to green and white. The floor is surprising, with its large beige and white tiles, but somehow it works.

GREEN BEDROOMS

One of the prettiest bedrooms I know achieves its style by bringing the outdoors inside. It is on the corner of an old English country house and its four deep Queen Anne windows look out over a walled garden. From the strategically placed bed, the rooks in the beech trees, the early-flowering cherry, the specimen trees, chosen for their variety of leaf and form, can all be admired whatever the season. Bedrooms should always make more of their views, if they are good ones, instead of draping the windows with layers of lace and chintz. Of course, most of us lack such a verdant outlook, but the point is that a changing vista of green can be calming as you lie in bed at the end of a long day and invigorating at the start of a new one. And this effect can be achieved in the decor if the view fails to provide it.

One good way to start is with the carpet, and what more natural than a deep grass-green to be walked over barefoot? Moving upward, a leafy wallpaper can simulate any scene from a forest glade to a bower of roses with only the occasional bud peeking out from a trellis of leaves. There are much sought-after Chinese wallpapers, imported to the West from the 17th century onward (but only recently successfully reproduced), which are painted with faraway hills and tall, angular, exotic trees with colourful birds of strange varieties perched on the branches. Intended to surround the sleeper with an idealized garden, a paper like this needs no ornament. Keep the chair covers to the plainest marbled green, hang no pictures and swag no drapes.

Up in the attics look for simple, single-coloured 19th-century wallpapers. Their soft greens and tiny leaf patterns are charmingly in keeping with such rooms – it was for them they were intended. Here, white and green painted wicker, rush or pine furniture, small in scale to suit the room, should be treated with tidiness and simplicity. On the walls nothing more is needed than one or two simple samplers or those collections of pressed grasses and flowers which 19th-century women were so expert at making. Do not assume that this is a country room. High up in the terraces of 19th-century urban America, Britain, France and Germany the same simplicity was being created and is still valued today. And because this was the period when society ladies were encouraged to paint watercolours of interiors, there are plenty to inspire the modern designer.

Bedrooms are the place for fragile or sentimental heirlooms: a needlepoint carpet sewn by an ancestor, perhaps, its green and white garlands too precious to be risked downstairs; an old screen of fading green damask or a hand-worked silk quilt embroidered with ivy. In the bedroom they can be appreciated daily by those who love them – and kept apart from those who know no better. Indeed, because bedrooms are always places of privacy, they are often where the most personal objects are kept and admired so it is sensible to create a little display of favourite china in a glass-fronted, built-in cabinet, perhaps itself painted with sprigs or leaves to match the grassy carpet. And on the walls, groups of watercolour landscapes can conjure up a dream of England before the Industrial Revolution, a grand tour of the Black Forest or the tree-clad Apennines.

Sometimes a bedroom must be made in a basement and here the trick is to beat the dark at its own game. Make a grotto of deep green walls with ferns bursting from printed drapes and growing on painted stands. Green glass shades to a host of small table lights will pick up and emphasize precious pieces in the gloom, while the carpet, just as dark, should be ankle-deep and totally luxurious. This is a room for midnight feasts, scented with ferny burning oils and full of mystery.

GREEN BATHROOMS

*T*here was a time, early in the 20th century, when everyone painted their bathrooms plain green. But what a shade – like old pea soup, it must have been the most uninviting bathroom decor ever and it gave the green bathroom a bad reputation. Generations of children swore that their bathrooms would be any colour but that and only now is green making a welcome return. When you choose your colour, think not of icehouse green but of tropical jungles or of sunlight slanting through the newly opened leaves of beech forests. Contrasted with the purest white, of tub, basin and thick fleecy towels, a leafy wallpaper turns bathtime into the purest pleasure.

Before modern heating and ventilation systems solved the problem, bathrooms were highly dangerous places for any decent picture or print (which would become sodden or foxed) or for any good piece of furniture, whose veneer would lift. Thus it was that clever people used pretty plates to decorate their bathrooms. Such schemes are still attractive, and those early 19th-century botanical plates, hand-painted on white grounds, look handsome arranged in tiers above the bathtub. But today prints or pictures can take their place. Once again, botanicals are the ideal choice, or perhaps those prints by the 19th-century artist George Baxter, who looked deep into the rainforests and found half-clothed maidens lounging by rockpools.

Houseplants are perfect in the green bathroom. Not clichés like the Swiss cheese plant or thick-leaved succulents, but the floppy-leaved houselime, so-called because its leaves are the same bright green as the lime tree, or scented beauties like the white-flowered jasmine. Other suitable plants are the climbing kangaroo vine, if kept pruned hard enough to stop it gangling, or strap-leaved orchids, as elegant without flowers as they are exotic with them. I like the idea, if space permits, of transforming the clinical shapes of bathroom fittings by arranging plants on wirework or cast-iron staging. Larger species – orange and lemon trees in decorative pots, olives, figs and even indoor palms – could also be massed together in a corner to make the green bathroom a conservatory.

But enough of jungles. Why not a 19th-century sprigged bathroom with little green sprays all over the wallpaper, complemented with green grosgrain ribbon along the edge of ceiling and dado? A room busy with green-painted *faux* bamboo chairs and towel rails, tole lights painted with leaves and at least one set of jug and ewer, soap dish and toothbrush holder, all sprigged too. If the bathroom is the big country-house type, comfortable tub chairs, needlework rugs of flowers and leaves worked in squares and some antique linen draped on towel rails make it the ideal place for getting ready for a smart party, so relaxed is its ambience.

The subtle tones of gray-green are explored in an elegantly serene and spacious bathroom which is light years away from the spartan approach favoured by our parents. This is a place in which to celebrate the unhurried pleasures of the tub – a room where, if the return to reality can be delayed still further, there are comfortable seats to while away an hour or two in companionable gossip. Pale patterns of green flowers and foliage in fabrics by Manuel Canovas cover the floor-length tablecloth and the two outer cushions or pillows on the sofa in a colour which refers to the darker drape in the foreground, as do the olive-coloured picture mounts. In contrast, the central sofa cushion and the drape at the window from the Designers Guild "Trees" collection take a bluer tone. Note – a witty touch – how the bushy papyrus heads on the table repeat the shape of the shaving brush perched at the end of the bathtub.

The White Anthology

A 19th-century print of the common arum or calla lily, **Zantedeschia aethiopica** (right). The genus was named after a 19th-century Italian botanist and this species, originally from South Africa, was naturalized in many frost-free regions worldwide, where it is happiest growing in water.

White diagrammatic flowers formally arranged on a strong inky blue-black background are an effective foil to the cool gray paint of this Paris bedroom (opposite). The fabric on the chair, an ikat and tartan hybrid, is Comoglio's "Tours". For the key to the fabrics on the previous pages, see page 187.

White flowers seem the most natural of all. It is from them that many of our cultivated, domestic blooms have come, often by crossing with other colours common in nature, such as yellow and pink. Of course, there are many cultivated double forms of white blossoms – lilac, camellia, rose and narcissus spring to mind – but most have avoided the fate of their more colourful sisters. They have not been inbred into ridiculous shapes or extraordinary variegations. They have kept their simple beauty and, very often, their meadow scents.

Is there a connection between this natural quality and the fact that so many white flowers have come to represent virginity, purity and goodness? Why is white in the West the colour that brides carry in their bouquets, the token of joy, whereas in the East it represents mourning?

The most important flower in the white spectrum must be the lily. Probably the oldest cultivated flowering plant in existence, it was grown in the gardens of Minoan Crete around 2800 BC as the royal flower, and the Egyptians made beads in the shape of lilies for necklaces worn by aristocratic ladies. The Syrians loved the Madonna lily and there is an ivory bedhead, now to be seen in the British Museum, dating from the eighth century BC, carved with genies who hold pine cones and buckets as they tend sacred trees surrounded by lilies. In Classical mythology the Erythraean sibyl held a lily and it is the emblem of as many Christian saints as the rose, among them Saints Clare, Euphemia and Scholastica, and Francis of Assisi and Thomas Aquinas. The Virgin Mary herself was known as the lily among thorns and, of course, the Madonna lily was her special attribute. The lily frequently appears in medieval and Renaissance paintings of the Annunciation, sometimes beside Mary and sometimes held by the Archangel Gabriel, for it was his flower too. However, if Gabriel is holding an olive branch, it is almost certainly correct to assume that the painting is by an artist from the Sienese school because the white lily was also the symbol of the city state of Florence, Siena's great rival. Ironically, Catherine of Siena is one of the nine saints whose emblem is the lily.

But the lily is not the only sign of innocence in Christian symbolism. The white daisy is another, although it is usually attributed to the Holy Child. Daisy tiles were also found in Egyptian decor and in Crete. In medieval times, daisies appeared in French *millefleurs* tapestries and were thrown into herbal salads. Even their roots were eaten, boiled, with the expectation that sweet dreams would follow.

In China the extraordinary reverence accorded to the flowering cherry amounted almost to worship. Around 600 to 900 AD craftsmen of the Tang dynasty were already embellishing their silverwork with its blossom. The white cherry, among the earliest of the spring-flowering trees and therefore known as one of the Three Friends of Winter, was a particular favourite of Chinese painters and calligraphers for many centuries.

The white-blossomed elder tree also had special properties. Elder was believed to be a plant which protected other plants, and people as well. The Russians say it drives away bad spirits, but there, as everywhere in northern Europe, it has to be treated with caution. In Britain, woods-men had to ask its permission before cutting it down or even pruning it, and in Denmark elder furniture is considered unlucky, especially for a cradle, and burning elder on a fire is said to bring death in its wake. More lightheartedly, an infusion of elder is traditionally known as a cure for freckles and elder wine is rightly famous for its flowery green taste.

Floral motifs in the pure white scalloped and draped lace and in the drawn-thread tablecloth add instant charm to a pretty alcove (opposite). A 19th-century print of a bloom then classified as Chrysanthemum *'Madame F. Sander' (above).*

The hawthorn was another plant which might bite back, perhaps because it had strong pagan connotations which the early Christians tried to stifle – by bad-mouthing it. Since before Christianity in Britain its blossom had been picked on May Day (hence its English common name, may) and used to decorate the house and welcome the spring. In the 17th century the diarist John Evelyn bewailed the damage still being done to the fine hawthorns in Woodstock Park near Oxford. But may was always witch ridden – I remember as a child being cautioned not to cut the blossom and arrange it in the house because it was bound to bring bad luck.

On the other hand, myrtle did nothing but good. Its white flowers are, apparently, common at cottage doors – I do not recall seeing any, but folklorists swear so. Myrtle always made up part of the bride's bouquet and the bridesmaids would take pieces from the posy and plant them. If the cutting flourished, the story went, the bridesmaid herself would soon be married. Of course, myrtle roots rather easily. A pinkish white is very flattering to the complexion, which may well be another reason why brides chose to carry myrtle blossom. Madame de Pompadour knew the value of that colour well for she insisted on decorating her rooms with a carefully chosen white and gilt. And you can still see a tiny Parisian panelled writing room of 1779 from the Hôtel Serilly in those same colours, decorated with scallop shells (attributed to Venus), the flower goddesses Flora, Pomona and Ceres and swags of white and gilded flowers.

Some of the commonest white wildflowers are members of the Umbelliferae family, many of them well used as herbs in the past. Chervil, also called sweet cicely, has a sweet aniseedy taste; lovage resembles hot celery; and aromatic angelica candies nicely. All three were also used against the plague and as strewing herbs, thrown on the floors of banqueting halls and chambers. Angelica was so named because an angel revealed to a monk that the herb would protect against the plague; in Lapland, poets were crowned with its hollow stems. Lovage was introduced to Britain by the Romans but now grows wild around the coast and, before spices were discovered and brought to the West, lovage seeds were used instead of pepper.

Meadowsweet, which was also called bride's wort in England because it was often carried by brides, is one of the loveliest of all wildflowers, growing in great creamy white clusters and sweetly scented with honey. It was also a favourite strewing herb; John Gerard, the 16th-century herbalist, wrote of it, "...the leaves and flowers of meadowsweet excel all other strong herbes for to deck up houses, to strew in chambers, halls and banqueting houses in the summer time; for the smell thereof makes the heart merrie and delighteth the senses." What a pity, comments the 20th-century herbalist Eleanour Sinclair Rohde, that the English office of King's (or Queen's) Herb Strewer has fallen into abeyance. "Dressing in a white gown and scarlet mantle with old lace, on her head a wreath of laurel and oak leaves and round her neck, her badge of office, she was attended by six maidens, attired in white adorned with flowers and greenery. And each pair carried between them a two-handled basket from which they strewed the herbs." Such an unlikely ceremony would undoubtedly add a certain something to state visits today.

In dark corners white arrangements can glow, set against brilliant colours they have startling clarity, and in cool company they keep their place. White, used judiciously, can make a surprisingly bold statement: (top left) lilies and chrysanthemums combine for studied simplicity in an all-white country-sophisticate interior; (top right) contrasting shapes and textures in a casual arrangement of cow parsley and snowberries; (bottom left) a formal arrangement of speckled lilies, greeny-white nicotiana and daisies for a Georgian hall;

(bottom right) lily heads taking most of the attention against the strong green walls but the marguerites at floor level help conceal an intrusive radiator; (opposite) jonquils and lilac, picked as it opened and ranging from pale green to brilliant white, are set against gray-green spikes of lavender and rosemary. Jonquils also look wonderful alone. I love rectangular glass tanks filled with great bunches of them – or of spring daffodils or narcissus – all in shades of the palest cream or white, their petals starting forward or slanting back.

WHITE ARRANGEMENTS

Certain flowers can stand the all-white treatment – notably Regale lilies, which look stunning if cut short and massed in huge circular bowls – but always check the effect, particularly when using chrysanthemums and arum lilies. Roses are perfect for small bouquets in living and dining rooms. The white flowers of philadelphus are scented and great sprays can be cut to make tall vases full of white and green. Another scented shrub for late spring arrangements is the evergreen Mexican orange, its white sprays surrounded by glossy green leaves. Its heavy fragrance means it is perhaps better suited to night-time appearances.

Informal arrangements for small rooms can include, as well as those adaptable roses, the ever-popular marguerites and ox-eye daisies. Scented lily of the valley is most often seen on breakfast or tea trays because it is so at home with silver.

White foliage is available too – furry gray and white lamb's lugs, perhaps, or the shrubby senecio. Variegated ivies and hollies also make excellent foils to white arrangements all year.

WHITE LIVING ROOMS

A white living room may, initially, seem improbable. But, of course, white comes in many shades. There are warm, pinky whites, cool greeny ones and all sorts of shades from stone to magnolia, depending on whether the red, blue, green or brown spectrums are mixed with it. And a great many of these whites will live happily together as long as they are carefully chosen. So the living room can sparkle with the brighter green or blue shades of white or become much mellower with the beiges and pale browns of old linen and paper.

A designer working on the interior of a grand Victorian house in San Francisco managed the trick perfectly when putting together a living room which breathes flowery elegance. Her whites, of course, are not strictly white at all. There is a fine French mantelpiece, all carved acanthus leaves and palmettes, of dull, creamy stone. The floor, of wooden planks, is lime-washed to the palest, streaked tan. The walls are panelled and plastered with floral motifs – bouquets of flowers and interlinking swags – all painted a neutral shade of beige and subtly washed to bring out the shadows of the carving. The curtains or drapes pick up exactly this colour and, because they are extremely full, shade the strong sunlight into a peachy glow. The upholstered wooden

White flowers lighten the darker side of this room (see also pages 137–9), in the fabrics, including the self-patterned daybed and tapestry chair (right), and in copious and charming arrangements (below).

armchairs are painted in the palest dove-gray while the fabric strews tiny pink roses and green leaves on a satiny white. Other cushions or pillows take up the floral theme, using similar fabric, alongside some of plain white lace and hemstitched old linen. A white room? It may not sound so, but it looks the part.

All this is very European. A living room in a Georgian townhouse in England can achieve the same flowery pallor by emphasizing fine architectural features. Cleaned and hollowed out, the impressed roses, acanthus leaves and anthemions of 18th-century ceiling mouldings become doubly important in a pale room, as do the little roundels of flowers carved on the corners of white marble fireplaces. Reed and round mouldings on built-in bookshelves and cupboards deserve the same attention. Most townhouses of this period will have good floorboards; slightly sanded and polished or limed white, they provide a good basis for the studied simplicity of the white room. On them fling stone-shaded rugs, their pile cut into flower patterns or woven with the very palest pink roses and daisies.

Upholstery in the white room should be one of a series of creams or beiges – self-patterned jacquards, bullion-fringed heavy linen or even fine wool, covered with an all-over diamond pattern and sprigs. Then, because the monochrome effect needs variety, the chairs should be liberally spread with cushions or pillows of faded chintz or tea-stained linen, hand-embroidered with pale brown flowers. And on quilt-covered side tables or marbled shelves, array plain glasses, painted with white silhouettes, silver rose-bowls or white marble busts of young girls, their hair wreathed in flowers.

In the country, the living room has to be much more practical. Faded chintzes are at home on giant sofas and easy chairs and plain wooden boards make good sense but curtains or drapes – which will not get spoiled by mud and dog – can take advantage of the cleaner air by being made of floating, heavily flowered white lace or sprigged voile. Pictures are unnecessary if there are enough architectural features in the room. And if none exist, add them. Ceiling medallions, plaster moulds of flowers and leaves, and wall lights like Grinling Gibbons' flower carvings, all washed with transparent light brown varnish, will give blank walls the detail they need.

Finally, to the white living rooms which suit the village houses of the Mediterranean so well. The walls are simply whitewashed and the floor is terracotta or the palest pink or creamy marble. Detail comes with a few fine pieces of furniture in light oak carved with bouquets or sprays of flowers and curly, pale-painted chairs. Stand huge green- or white-glazed pots of greeny white flowers on pale pink terracotta plinths or tiny white marble tables and this is a room in which to idle away the hottest afternoon or sultry evening.

The huge spaces of a London room designed to be an artist's studio would not, at first sight, seem to lend themselves to white, especially given the deliberately formal style the designer has adopted – the dangers of coldness are all too obvious. But the decorative painter Hannerle Dehn has assembled so many subtle shades, patterns and textures that the effect of her pale scheme is lush rather than spartan. Note particularly the charming sofa: on a damask patterned with white floral garlands, she has painted free-flowing trails of leaves and flowers which parallel the rich embroidery on the floor-length tablecloth nearby.

WHITE DINING ROOMS & KITCHENS

*T*here was a time in the 1960s when virtually every room was stripped of its decorative features and painted a stark white. That everyone lived inside plain white cubes made decorating less stressful but it swiftly led to a reaction. White rooms, or at any rate plain white rooms, are now quite rare. This is especially true of dining rooms, which tend to be richly coloured, and the disappearance of starched white linen and damask has removed even the snowy expanses of the tablecloth.

Is it time to give the pale dining room its turn again? To make eating the more formal affair it was in the Georgian period? A long oval or rectangular table, lined with chairs, was expected to groan with silver, white double-damask napkins neatly arranged on each white plate, while a whole series of greater and lesser cut-crystal glasses stood beside each place. The room was decorated with a wallpaper, or even the self-patterned silk which Florence and Rome still excel in, whose white background was sprigged with off-white flowers. Great tazzas of porcelain or silver held bunches of white-candied grapes, and, for really great occasions, 18th-century cooks made whole gardens from spun white sugar.

It is possible to re-create this atmosphere in miniature. White, flower-woven tablecloths and napkins are readily available, while, with clever purchasing, silver flatware is no more expensive than modern plate, and white flowers for the table are no problem. Grapes and other fruit can be frosted with sugar and the old practice of garnishing food with flowers should be revived – try daisies, white elderflowers and the heads of sweet cicely. Use candles in plain glass holders if silver is not to hand and chandeliers or wall sconces with mirrored facets cut with petals. The china should also be white, with elegantly drawn borders of pale flowers or Florentine curlicues its only decoration. Jugs of mineral water floating with flowers or even flower cordials or wines – mint, elderflower again, or lemon – should stand, fresh from the refrigerator, around the table.

When devising such splendour, remember one cardinal rule. White in the dining room is at its best when the table is the focus of attention, and you should be uncompromising – white here means true bright white. The rest of the room, in daylight or candlelight, looks best when shaded toward a creamy off-white.

There is another version of the white dining room which works well in urban settings because white can have a calming influence. Again, the combination of fabric, silver and crystal is used, but this time flounces of pretty lace, small bouquets of drooping white roses and the daintiest white incised china give the dining room a flavour of the boudoir. Perfect, of course, for dinners *à deux*, but also relaxing for old-fashioned tea parties, this is a room for cucumber sandwiches in the thinnest white bread served with Lapsang tea at four o'clock.

Floral schemes in period style do not have to be complex or even cluttered. The white-flowered motif on a pale ground which appears yellowed with age in this handsome but simple 18th-century dining room at the Morris-Jumel Mansion in New York might have been stencilled, so regular and stylized is the pattern of flowers interspersed with sprays of grasses arranged in stripes. In fact, it is a printed fabric, "Algernon" by Raintree Designs. Its charm owes much to the style of colonial America, as do many of the elements in this scheme. The soft green of the dado and paintwork arrived in 18th-century America via Scandinavia, as did the habit of painting floorcloths. The American Federal furniture includes an elegant set of chairs by Duncan Phyfe.

WHITE BEDROOMS & BATHROOMS

*B*edrooms lend themselves to the all-white treatment. Beds – those huge blocks of white – always have to be cossetted and cajoled to look good so, if their whites can gently blend with the whites around them, the problem is solved. Modern fashion dictates that beds should not be disguised by counterpanes or quilts but that the bed linen itself should be so beautiful and so carefully considered that it needs no cover.

Both modern and antique pillow cases can be found which revel in flowery lace and embroidery. Frilled, flounced, appliquéd and embroidered, there is a wonderful choice of all-white covers. It is also easy to find bed pillows of all shapes and sizes – any will make a background to a huge array of cushions or decorative pillows of descending size. Each one should be covered with white cotton or linen, each a different texture or design. For bedding, a great soft feather duvet is preferable, vastly oversized. The valance continues the white, flouncy theme – not lace this time, but perhaps parts of an old white damask tablecloth whose middle has seen better days but whose flower-bordered edges can be re-used here.

The extravagant multicoloured curtains or drapes of recent years may be starting to pall but the all-white look still lends itself to ruched and swagged styles draped over curtain poles and caught with tie-backs. Use lengths and lengths of white flowery lace and voile, thickly gathered but still translucent, with the ends trailing elegantly on the floor. The bed, if you are lucky enough to have a four-poster, can be treated the same way.

All-white rooms have to be planned with care. If every single piece of furniture, every cushion or pillow and curtain or drape were exactly the same tone of white, the effect would be as disorientating as a snow storm. But, while bright colours should not be introduced, it is possible to get away with neutrals in a white bedroom. Curly black iron chairs, covered with white lace cushions or pillows, can be placed to direct the eye. Silver-topped perfume bottles or candelabra with white parchment shades will add glitter and richness. Monochrome drawings and prints, framed in silver, look good on the walls.

This bedroom is, of course, hardly Minimalist despite its discipline. But white is equally at home with Modernism or country-cottage style. The Modernist approach is to dispense with virtually everything – no bed, only a futon or mattress on the floor, no cupboards or closets but those which are built-in and invisible, no paintings, nothing but black and white. One eccentric chair is allowed and a bunch of exotic blooms.

The country-cottage white bedroom is more friendly. Starting with plain, lime-washed walls and relying on only a few pieces of near-black oak furniture (in an all-white room, black is acceptable), the comfort comes from one of those beautiful old crocheted cotton bedspreads, made in squares with a chunky, bobbly texture. A towel-horse carries an assortment of hand towels edged with tatting and, on the chest of drawers, a carefully worked white traycloth with a little pottery ornament.

When I think of an all-white bathroom, then Italy comes to mind, perhaps because there they have never been seduced by all that ultra-thick, multicoloured towelling or by bathtubs and basins in such unlikely colours as avocado and chocolate. The Italians have kept their bathrooms old-fashioned (apart from hotels in Milan, that is) and it is still the norm to be given the unfluffy white towels that were once common all over Europe.

So I think of white-washed walls and pale marble floors, a simple iron bath on feet and, white on white, towel-horses full of damask and linen, perhaps with patterns of daisies or ivy woven into the fabric. Some of the towels will have cotton-lace edges. More figured linen or a heavy lace with stylized flowers woven around its hems will be used for the curtains or drapes, which will, of course, be blowing gently in a sunny breeze.

This may be a daydream, but a simple white room such as this can easily be created, especially if all the mundane cosmetics and potions can be hidden away, in a plain white cupboard or closet, naturally. It is not at all difficult to find old linen towels, and modern bathmats, bathsheets and flannels are all made in white. Continue the pristine look with pure white herbal soaps or off-white bars of Marseilles soap, softened with olive oil.

White, being the colour of purity, is very attractive in a room devoted to hygiene – why else did Estée Lauder call a scent "White Linen"? – so the white bathroom should smell cool and fresh. There are numerous sharp colognes, including the old-fashioned "4711", and toilet waters based on the greenish white flowers of the orange or lemon tree.

The white bathroom makes other demands too. It must always be warm and welcoming – a cold room of this sort would instantly seem bleak. It must also be utterly disciplined. Every flannel, every towel, every object must conform. If you add a mug of red toothbrushes or quantities of colourful pictures on the walls, the room will be white no longer. Worse still, none of these flowery whites must lose its brightness or become discoloured. If such a rigorous regime is for you, you will have a room which reinvigorates every morning and calms every night.

An antique counterpane richly embroidered with stylized white flowers and trailing foliage complements the cool blue of the panelled and painted walls of this elegant French 18th-century bedroom. The pink roses, the darker furniture and even the sheen of old satin all add warmth to the scheme. Note the foliage decoration on the head and base of this handsome bed – plain bedheads can easily be decorated with mouldings and then colour-washed to match a scheme.

*Flowery linen and old lace dress a pretty 19th-century white-painted cast-iron bed (right), its white expanses softened by the cleverly judged off-whites of the floral self-patterned damask on the sofa at its end, which is piled deep with embroidered and lacy cushions or pillows. There is floral lace at the left-hand window too and a particularly fine fragment has been mounted and hung beside it. The multiple flower prints above the bed are another floral element, but they also help to organize what could have been a slightly bitty arrangement. Note the pale, honey-golden marbling on the ceiling moulding and the lower panels of the cupboard or closet, another strategy for breaking up large areas of plain white. This is a romantic room, the wall muralled with **amaretti** and the ceiling with swags of flowers, while heart-shaped wreaths hang above the bed. Nina Campbell's "Artois Stripe", a white-rose chintz designed for Osborne & Little (above), is mellowed with a pale yellow ribbon motif. The antique ivory-backed brushes and pots on the frilled dressing table continue the off-white theme but another, more acceptable addition to the white bedroom in today's enlightened climate are the lustrous old photograph frames, made of mother-of-pearl. Flower-decked silver frames would work just as well.*

The
Multicoloured
Anthology

Sharp citrus-yellow tones and dark blood-red roses make the boldest statements in a room where textiles carry much of the burden of the multicoloured floral theme (opposite). Note how the off-white walls balance what could easily have become a cluttered room.

Striped and ragged parrot tulips such as these exotic examples (left) were first bred in Europe by Dutch plantsmen in the 17th century. They became so popular that the term "tulipomania" was coined to describe the speculation that ensued. For the key to the fabrics on the previous pages, see page 187.

*F*lora was the Roman goddess of flowers. She had her own festival, the Floralia, which, like much else in ancient Rome, was a good excuse for an orgy. Her Greek counterpart was Chloris, married to Zephyrus, god of the west wind, and she was said to follow on her husband's heels to bring the buds to full bloom. Botticelli's painting of spring, *La Primavera*, now in the Uffizi Gallery in Florence, shows flowers flooding from the lips of Chloris as she turns into Flora, after being embraced by Zephyrus. This, one of the best-loved pictures in the world, was probably painted in 1482 to celebrate Lorenzo di Pierfrancesco de' Medici's marriage. It shows no less than 42 kinds of plants, nearly all flowering, which grew in the Tuscan hills in spring. Among them are carnations and daisies, cornflowers and periwinkles, and at her hip, Flora carries roses to strew beneath a grove of orange trees. The oranges were Botticelli's homage to his patron, whose heraldic symbol was six golden balls.

The fertile hills of Greece and Italy must account for the abundance of flowers in Classical mythology. The poet Virgil in the *Iliad*, describing Zeus bedding Hera on Mount Ida, says of the field on which they lay "the sacred earth brought forth fresh-sprouting grass and dewy clover and crocus and hyacinth, thick and tender, which raised them above the ground. There they lay and covered themselves in a beautiful golden cloud from which shining dewdrops fell." And in the *Odyssey* Homer writes of the garden of Alcinous, King of Phadeacia, with its beds of herbs, apples, vines, pomegranates, oranges and lemons, fed by two springs of water, and of the citrus plants' ability to fruit and flower simultaneously.

Flowers have also inspired some of the most beautiful mythological paintings. Included in any such list must be Flora dancing in her garden and strewing flowers, as depicted by the 17th-century French artist Nicolas Poussin, and several portraits of his wife, Saskia, as the goddess Flora by Poussin's Dutch contemporary, Rembrandt. The Venetian painters Francesco Guardi and Pietro Longhi both hired beautiful prostitutes for the role, Flora often being shown with chubby cherubs.

With little sense of irony, the Christian Church managed to amalgamate and transform Flora and the frequently flower-bedecked goddess of love, Venus, into the Virgin Mary. Her ethereal looks matched Venus' own and she was often surrounded by as many flowers. She appears with the unicorn, a symbol of virginity, on fields of spring flowers in medieval and Renaissance tapestry and on Italian brides' marriage chests. More than 100 varieties of flowers were embroidered onto the French early 16th-century "Lady and the Unicorn" tapestries, which can still be seen at the Musée de Cluny in Paris, and most are perfectly recognizable. Similar fields of flowers appear on both male and female clothes, upholstery and bedhangings. All probably reflect an earlier fashion for gardens which were little more than contrived meadows. Unlike the "wild gardens" which are tended so carefully today, these charmingly named "flowering meads" were lawns sown with low-growing flowers like violets, primroses, pinks and daisies – the effect can be seen in an altarpiece by the 15th-century Flemish artists Hubert and Jan van Eyck, *The Adoration of the Lamb*, in Ghent cathedral.

Despite this interest in nature, the still life, as frescoed on the walls of Pompeii and constructed in mosaics on Roman pavements everywhere, died out almost completely in the Christian era until the 16th century. When the genre reappeared in northern Europe (the word actually comes from the Dutch *stilleven*), many of the paintings were religious, taking the attributes of the Holy Family and the saints and arranging them in significant relationships to one another. Today the meanings are often obscure. The Virgin might be shown as an olive tree, pomegranate, lily, apple or orange; Joseph might also be a lily, or a flowering staff; the Holy Ghost, a columbine; and the three-lobed clover leaf might represent the Trinity. Other paintings were intended to remind viewers of the brevity of human life, mixing candles with butterflies and skulls with flowers. Later, in the grand 17th- and 18th-century fruit and flower setpieces, French artists such as Nicolas Robert were commissioned by royalty. Robert painted the specimens in the botanical gardens at Blois for Gaston d'Orleans, and his *Florilegium* would be found in many wealthy homes of the period. Jean-Baptiste Monnoyer later decorated Versailles and other French palaces with setpiece oil paintings, going on to design wallpaper, borders and tapestry

A 19th-century French print of carnations, long bred for their candy stripes. "Bizarre" varieties – two colours on a white ground – were then the most prized. Other types included one-colour streaks on white and coloured spots on a white or yellow ground.

for Beauvais and Gobelin. Such paintings were highly artificial since the blooms were always immaculate and arranged with careful symmetry; no doubt late 17th-century interiors were full of real vases of real flowers on plinths doing their best to keep up with the paintings. In the work of the Dutch flower painters Jan van Huysum and his father Justus only the butterflies of the early paintings survived. They gloried in huge pyramids of roses, tulips, convolvulus, grapes, pomegranates and apricots set in Classical urns, often delaying completion of a picture for many months to capture the fruits of several seasons as they matured.

The golden age of floral design began in the 17th century when, alongside these still lifes, floral patterns appeared as marquetry on clocks and chests, and were sewn into huge tapestries and knotted into small table carpets. Artists of the 18th century, such as the French Jean-Baptiste Siméon Chardin and Jean-Baptiste Oudry, reacted against the heady exuberance of the van Huysums with quiet displays of kitchen herbs or vegetables. But by then floral designs were also appearing on fine porcelain, on jewellery and on multi-coloured chintzes and Oriental rugs.

It is strange that the flowering of Indian art, which still influences Western decor today, should have begun with the descendants of Tamburlaine and Genghis Khan, but the Mughal rulers who conquered India in the 16th century were great lovers of nature. The first, Babur, wrote poems about the spring flowers of the Hindu Kush whereas his grandson, Akbar, imported carpet makers and painters. Akbar's hall of private audience, covered with 1,000 rugs, was said to resemble "a beautiful flowerbed", his tent walls were lined with chintz and he also encouraged the making of Kashmir shawls.

However, it was not until the last quarter of the 17th century that the East-West trade in fabrics really got going, and by 1700 the craze for complete room sets had developed, using matching or coordinated chintz for curtains or drapes, bedhangings and walls. This, alongside the fashion for printed wallpapers and the new Oriental rugs, created a style which is still popular today. At first, tree of life patterns on cotton bedhangings, wallhangings and floorspreads were the most popular, but later Chinoiserie and the influence of European design through the East India companies contrived to create the amalgam which is the colourful floral chintz of today.

Multicoloured floral decor offers endless freedom for spontaneous still lifes which can be quickly formed and re-formed to suit the mood, the season or the occasion. Blue tones and Chinoiserie unite a seemingly haphazard juxtaposition of **toile** wallpaper, chintz, ironstone pottery, porcelain and glass (top left); only the little green flask strikes a defiant note. Note the delightful leaf pattern around the edge of the table. A tea or coffee tray can bring another temporary element to the chemistry of the floral room: clearly the red anemones on the silver tray (top right) recall a faded cotton quilt to its former bright shade but the floral theme is reinforced by motifs on the plate, whereas the porcelain (bottom left) finds echoes in the blue of the paisley sofa and the Chinese inlay table. Behind the same sofa, another inlay table, from India, is home for several inlay pieces decorated with floral motifs (bottom right), including a **pietra dura** box. Indian inlay of this quality is an attractive way to add stylized floral patterns to any scheme.

MULTICOLOURED ARRANGEMENTS

U ntil recently, nearly all modern flower arrangements were multicoloured, complex in conception and large in scale. Today the fashion is for something simpler. But although many vases are now filled with single-colour arrangements, a different approach confines the blooms to one species so that their shapes are largely the same while their colours vary.

The obvious flower to use is the rose, but anemones create the same full-blown effect in spring. Lilies are now available all year and a few stalks of mixed bold colours are extremely dramatic. The light can be so bright in high summer that even more colourful arrangements of mixed herbaceous species are permissible. But, when making your choice, balance bold patches of colour with each other and take care to vary the forms of the plants. Come winter, there are coloured berries (white snowberry, red hollies and black ivy heads) and stems (bright red, green and yellow from cornus) to make use of, while selections of coloured ivy work well in dark corners.

A half-glazed terracotta pot filled with red sweet williams, sweet-scented white stocks and purple anemones (left) has a country simplicity which matches the leaf- and flower-stencilled walls, while the pewter tankard of white sweet williams, pale pink roses and blue daisies (right) refers to the sprigged and sponged pottery ranked on the shelves of a distressed and colour-washed kitchen dresser. The flat-headed sweet william – a long-time favourite in cottage gardens – also looks good with tendrils of ivy and the multicoloured spikes of hybrid lupins.

A dish full of polished lemons and a shallow bowl find an echo in an arrangement of roses, delphiniums, narcissus and rosemary (opposite). The simple trick of placing flowers before a mirror instantly doubles the size of an arrangement. Multicoloured roses grouped alone in a glass jug or silver bowl look equally good in high summer. White, pink, scarlet, bright yellow and apricot – such a mixture of buds and blooms, along with the best, freshest leaves, is invariably charming.

One useful strategy in a multicoloured arrangement is to separate the primary colours in different vases (left). Here one vase mixes the bright yellow of golden rod and red gladioli, while another holds blue cornflowers and white viburnum. Foliage can also help to cool bold patches of colour. For example, the silvery gray leaves of the multiflowered yellow senecio will tone down a pairing with the feathery pink astilbe, with perhaps just a sprinkling of ox-eye daisies.

All the primary colours are used in an arrangement which crams the vivid colours and strong, tight shapes of zinnias and dahlias from the red and yellow spectrum into a blue and white pottery trough with equal presence (left). But multicoloured arrangements can be restrained, as in the lighthearted mixture of scarlet azaleas, white narcissi and blue columbines (right) created for a largely red and white room; a group of angular, spiky petalled lilies – pink-spotted, purest white and purple or fiery orange – would look equally good in this formal setting.

MULTICOLOURED LIVING ROOMS

*I*s your taste for floral rooms where discipline is relaxed, where reds can riot alongside greens, blues with yellows, or glorious mixtures of any colour are allowed? To be successful, this kind of floral decor must be clever. Take decorator John Fowler's grand English country-house drawing rooms, for example. Co-founder of the design company Colefax and Fowler, his working life spanned the 1930s to 1960s. The chintzes and papers, the ambience he created, are now part of the company's stock in trade (if it will allow so humble a description of its work). It is a style which depends for its success on the mixing of floral patterns, sometimes several at a time, with plains and geometrics. Since the company designs its own fabrics, it can make sure that even the busiest combinations are calmed by certain thematic colours.

Such a living room can be achieved without so august a decorator, but it does help to stick to the output of one firm or one designer. For example, English decorator Geoffrey Bennison's various faded tea-rose patterns, pepped up by indigo or black, rub along very happily together. However, in the multicolour context the use of faded fabrics is, perhaps, cheating.

For real riots of colour, look at the work of Paris-based Manuel Canovas, who works the spectrum like a maestro and without any compromise. His fabrics and designs succeed because he gives colour a great deal of thought – he lives with swatches of pure tone, sifting and adjusting them, before embarking on an amalgam. Those who want to create brightly coloured complex floral living rooms should follow his example. Invest in a pinboard, take a series of swatches of favourite florals, plains, tickings, even tartans, and try them out together. The most surprising juxtapositions seem to work.

John Stefanides, another spirited colourist, enjoys mixing the busiest floral chintz with tartan. He believes tartan's square patterns give a better contrast than a simple plain fabric because they are more assertive. Etro of Milan has found the same. This firm also mixes energetic paisleys with great riots of roses in velvets, suedes, cottons and wools.

Potter Mary Rose Young, whose cottage in England is a true riot of primary colours, is another who demonstrates that mixed floral schemes are not limited to the traditional flowery chintzes. She created her living room from a mixture of shades inspired by North Africa. As her work shows, the Post-Modernist interior sets the primary colours in almost jarring conjunctions. But, to compensate, this style keeps clutter to a minimum and sticks to

Even in a multicoloured scheme where the flowers have been allowed to riot and every fabric is different, reds tend to dominate. The striped chairs play an essential part in holding this look together.

stark, simple shapes for rugs, furniture and fireplaces. It is inexpensive to achieve but requires an excellent eye and the discipline to edit out detail.

The country-house multicoloured style also requires discipline. Where a plain blue room can support a riot of different pictures and whole tablefuls of multicoloured marble objects, this will certainly not work in a room which is itself full of colours. One exception are those 19th-century mementoes of Queen Victoria's love affair with Scotland: tartan-clad Mauchline ware, named after the town where it was made, is now busily collected in Britain for massing on tabletops.

However, for many people black is a safer, and more pleasing, option. This is where simple black and white prints, massed in old ribbed black frames, will provide a sense of order. Or try dark bronze objects, black-painted iron doorstops and the like. Black papier mâché work – trays, fire screens, even little desks and chairs – looks wonderful against busy chintzes, the ornate shapes emphasized by a patterned background and the pretty mother-of-pearl flowers just taking away any severity.

White, like black, also brings calm to a busy room. Try antique tablecloths in flowered lace or whitework with appliquéd or cut-work edgings on fireside tables full of old silver, the finest lace curtains or drapes hung inside one of the hectic florals, or plain white porcelain in the Chinese manner. Or take one colour from the many and exploit it. For example, if you choose turquoise, you could search out those blue glass hyacinth vases made in the 19th century or elegant Chinese pottery, glazed and impressed with flowers. This kind of treasure hunt is fun and it gets results.

Another style of living room using a mix of floral colours is what I think of as the New York smart apartment look. It brings together a catholic mixture of objects – a stone buddha's head, a Tang camel, a whole series of African or pre-Columbian carvings – set against stark walls lacquered a Chinese red or Greek blue. The floral interest comes with the introduction of Oriental screens or wallhangings of whole gardens of flowers and greenery, and every horizontal surface is crowded with exotic vases of real flowers, especially those chosen for their architectural shapes, such as strelitzia or lilies, while great trees – olives, figs or house limes – stand in antique bronze vases. It is a curiously restful style but, unlike the English cottage, it is one which needs a great deal of money (or a worldwide search for acceptable replicas) to achieve.

Proof, if it were needed, that choosing the right fabrics is only part of the story: multicoloured floral themes need careful thought when dressing the rest of the room. Note the stack of hat boxes covered with floral paper, flower portraits, flowered trays and ceramics – this wild ensemble was built slowly piece by piece.

Mary Rose Young stands traditional decor on its head in her country dining room (right). Whereas walls and floor would normally be patterned, she stays strictly plain, leaving both decoration and the multicolours for a lively outside door and for the pottery on the blue-painted dresser. Around the door climbs flowering honeysuckle, while each of its four panels bears a spire of pinky foxgloves. Her pottery uses more stylized floral and vegetable motifs, plus animals – all in the brightest of palettes. Although this look is thoroughly modern, she has clearly been influenced by the paintings of Duncan Grant and Vanessa Bell (see page 22) and also by the pottery of their son, Quentin Bell. You could also plan a family kitchen around simple peasant furniture – bright painted chairs, their green slats strewn with daisies, hanging cupboards of red and blue, yellow shelves, little tables and children's pieces.

At first glance, this New York dining room (opposite) seems ablaze with all the colours of the Chinese palette, but the decorator has cleverly confined this effect to the wall surfaces above the dado and then reduced the area still farther with an elegant 18th-century gray and gilded mirrored closet. The same neutral paint tones appear on the Hepplewhite dining chairs and most of the woodwork. In an added touch of opulence, parts of the mouldings around the door to the room have been gilded but the picture frames, also gold, have been kept utterly simple. The fabric is a modern reproduction by Manuel Canovas from what is called a "period document" – in other words the source is either a period pattern book or a scrap of an original. Note how the flowers in the arrangement – including lilies, chrysanthemums and larkspur – echo the colours on the wall; dark ferns provide a backdrop.

MULTICOLOURED DINING ROOMS & KITCHENS

For some time now, the smartest family kitchens have been in the peasant style. The alternative fashion, Minimalism, works well in a small space but in a large room used to cook, to eat and for family living the atmosphere needs to be comfortable.

To my mind, the floral style that is happiest here is exemplified by the Provençal prints of the French company Souleiado – every one of them a riot of colour, their complex but far from naive patterns derived from a palette of primaries. These exuberant fabrics, and others like them developed throughout southern France, were originally inspired by equally vibrant cloths imported into Marseilles from India.

The multicoloured floral family kitchen, therefore, might use a cotton covered with exotic pink, blue and green flowers and leaves on a strong yellow ground for the tablecloth and as curtains to screen built-in, but naive, kitchen cabinets. Behind chicken wire, such fabric could hide the ketchup bottles and soy sauce that are far from peasant food. Then another pattern, perhaps a yellow and rose paisley on indigo, could take up the theme on covers and cushions or pillows.

This is a room which, in time, will furnish itself as all those oddments collected over the years build up. Such accretions need discipline at the least, but spicing the mix with folk art can bring coherence. English folk style was no less colourful than the French by the 19th century. Think of the bright fairground trinkets made by the Staffordshire potteries, charming barge ware with impressed flower bouquets stuck onto plain brown pots, or painted tole ware, again with great gaudy flowers. These pieces were inspired by the peasant traditions of Eastern Europe. The United States took up this inheritance with the great waves of immigrants it received throughout the 19th century, and in time developed the characteristic Pennsylvania ware – painted tin and wooden objects such as water jugs and brackets. The earlier pioneers had used their ingenuity to create works of beauty: rag rugs out of old clothes and blankets, their middles filled with floral bouquets, pictures from scraps and dried flowers, and frames, boxes and screens covered with remnants of floral wallpaper. Make that spirit your keynote as you create this most relaxed of rooms.

Mediterranean pottery would be quite at home here too. Portuguese heavy white ware, patterned with yellow and pink flowers, or the Italian white-based pottery which mixes blue, white and bright yellow shapes to form convoluted floral swags and stems around cartouches and lozenges in the medieval maiolica tradition. French *faïence* is lighter and prettier, with delicate roses and marguerites matched with plain plates of yellow or green, their floral designs impressed and barely hinted at. Each country makes giant soup tureens, big flowery jugs for lashings of table wine and chargers for fruit and salads.

Laying the table can be an art too. One day, perhaps, the theme will be green with vine-leaf dishes, green tumblers and great bunches of herbs in green vases. Another day, take blue and white and yellow – blue and white Staffordshire china, white mugs, yellow Provençal napkins and a yellow cloth, decorated with daisies, marguerites and cornflowers. Forget about Minimalism and just let all those colours sing out.

176

MULTICOLOURED BEDROOMS

*B*edrooms should not be stark. They must exude comfort, a sense that here is a place you can go to relax or sleep deeply. For me peace means long vistas from deep, rose-framed windows and the "sound" of a night-time silence, broken by the first noise of morning, the dawn chorus. But such peace is often not possible in the fumes and noise of big cities so bedrooms should try to re-create the ambience of rolling green meadows, the cypress-punctuated Tuscan hills or the scented and colourful lavender fields of France.

How to do this? Well, these country havens all have strong perfumes. Rarely as simple as pure lavender or rose, they are instead the mingled scents of new-mown hay, June-flowering yellow broom, honeysuckle, peach blossom and boxwood. This freshness can be re-created by placing bunches of mint or honeysuckle around the room, hanging pomanders beside clothes and laying underwear in new-lined drawers with nosegays of fresh or dried herbs according to season.

The impression of peace can be subliminal too. If the room looks a part of that country freshness, those who see it will unconsciously relax and feel less fraught. For example, perhaps you could combine bedspreads decorated with the full, ripe ears of wheat or barley and meadow-red poppies, walls covered with a paper of rampant climbing roses and a carpet the bright, clear green of new grass. The bedroom which relies on a mixture of floral patterns and colours often suggests the wildflowers of the roadside or the cottage garden with no colour scheme other than abundance.

Wallpapers and fabrics showing simple country flowers generally have one thing in common – they are placed on a neutral, white or cream background, on which the flowers can be appreciated. It makes sense to stick to this one constant. If the colours and shades are chosen with an artist's eye and deployed on a plain ground, their riotous effect is somewhat controlled. Look, for example, at the brightly coloured paintings of Elizabeth Blackadder, an English artist who grows bright tulips, lilies and irises for her work.

However, it is equally possible to make several bold colours work together. A perfect scarlet and yellow are strong companions, but, tempered with white, are perfectly at ease. Blue, white, ultramarine, purple and green, the colours of the

Blues and the mellower reds have been skilfully balanced in this elegant, multicoloured 18th-century basement bedroom in San Francisco. The unusual use of French Chinoiserie toile *on the ceiling as well as the walls contrives to make this large room a warm and intimate place. The influences are multi-ethnic too – the bedhangings are bright Indian cottons, the carpet Persian and the sofa paisley-inspired.*

blue herbaceous border, are soothing, as are all the varied sugared-almond shades of petunias or sweet peas.

Of course, bedrooms need decoration. What pictures should you hang, what furniture choose and what objects collect? One hugely busy bedroom I know, all complicated floral wallpaper in bright shades with curtains or drapes, four-poster hangings and quilt to match, somehow kept control by covering the walls with black silhouettes – with one extra-large set marching around the room just under the ceiling moulding. Another had a block of foxed old lithographs on the main wall and yet a third posed a huge landscape oil painting above the bed as a focal point. Simple oak, mahogany or walnut furniture can also contribute to the success of the multicoloured floral bedroom, providing an anchor in a hectic scheme.

Prettier rooms rely not on black but white. Huge curtains or drapes of the finest cotton voile can be loosely bunched to filter the light and contribute an airy sense of space. While everything around – carpet, curtains or drapes, walls – is busy with flowers, leaves and colour, the bed itself can remain an island of pure white, headed with ruched old linen caught at the apex by antique coronets or wreaths, and so can the chairs, painted white, plain wicker, or limed windsors.

The clever decorator achieves an effect not by a blow between the eyes, but by building, little by little, the right mood. That subliminal base of scent and the freshness of white fabric underpin the flounce or drama of the colourful whole. They may not be noticed by the visitor, or appreciated, day after day, by the sleeper but they are important just the same.

Multicoloured floral schemes work equally well using the softer tones of the spectrum, as demonstrated in a grand "mansion" apartment bedroom in New York (left and right), which has been reconstructed in the lighthearted Rococo style of a fashionable French bedroom of the late 18th century. Most of the fabrics in the room are modern reproductions from period documents. The canopied bed à la polonaise is dressed in a pretty striped and flowered Belgian cotton. Mounted high on the walls are charming hand-painted floral garlands and pastoral scenes on silk panels. The great cabbagey blooms on the mantelpiece are silk, made in Italy and chosen to echo the colours on the floor-length cloth thrown over the table nearby. The ranks of engravings which cover much of the walls are fashion plates from **Galerie du Mode,** *published in the reign of Louis XVI, and collected piece by piece.*

In her second bathroom (right) Mary Rose Young goes for a relatively restrained multicoloured floral effect. Ceramic roses play the part of handles or pulls on a roughly daubed old chest which now serves as a base for the wash basin or sink. Around them, she has painted simple green leaves in a witty variation on the traditions of European folk art. The handles, the vase and the clutch of sweet peas all take their colours from the bright tones of the roughly striped wall surface. Flowery handles or pulls are an ideal way to add permanent floral detail to a room. A more traditional scheme might include white china knobs painted with delicate sprigs or bouquets of flowers that coordinate with the design chosen for the curtain fabric or wallpaper. In winter, a generous bowl of potpourri (see page 28 for recipes) is an attractive alternative to the jug of sweet peas. Chose musky soaps to complement it.

Mary Rose Young's principal bathroom (opposite) gives flowers a dominant role. Hand-painted standard ceramic tiles create a fantasy dado where multicoloured fish graze on a seabed thick with flowering plants. The mirror is framed by a circle of curling ceramic leaves and even the chain or pull is threaded with trailing cloth to resemble seaweed. The same colours are used for the geometrical patterns on almost every other surface. Such abandon leaves the eye to enjoy the traditional square lines of the white basin or sink. Strikingly vivid, such a scheme would warm and cheer the chilliest or darkest bathroom. If your taste is more traditional, decorate the walls with brightly coloured reproductions of 19th-century floral tiles, paint great garlands of leaves and creeping plants on the pipes and cistern and seek out a pretty antique mirror decorated with flowers.

MULTICOLOURED BATHROOMS

When bathrooms first became common, we thought of them as sanitary places which, like hospital rooms, should be kept clinical. Most of the surfaces were covered with gloss paint, which could easily be washed down to eradicate the germs. As a result, bathrooms were bleak places, and people, especially children, were disinclined to wash very often. Now that this attitude has begun to change, bathrooms are allowed to be places of comfort, and luxury and colour are breaking out all over. For example, there is nothing inherently *wrong* with bright Indian floral cottons for bathroom curtains or drapes, or massed towels of midnight-blue, lemon-yellow and lime-green. The carpet underfoot does not really have to be plain – it can be as flowered and fancy as anything in the living room.

Why not, while you are at it, have a huge floral wallpaper – a thing of vigour, a touch exotic – or one of those ribbon and rose patterns so at home in English drawing rooms? Or you could treat the whole room as a conservatory with fabrics, objects and papers taking the place of the climbing plants: a paper of yellow roses climbing up a trellis, curtains or drapes of trellis pattern and a set of white wicker chairs, made comfortable with squabs upholstered in a green ferny design. The floor could be tiled in white, its edges patterned to match the tiles on the bathtub splashback, and covered for comfort with a rag rug or a mat sewn with crewelwork ferns and flowers.

If the bathroom is fairly small – or you moderately rich – what more enjoyable than converting it into a Chinese room? Papers, hand-painted with plants, flowers, birds, insects and love scenes,

were brought to Europe from China in the 17th century and quickly became the rage. Today they are being reproduced in more manageable sizes. With a dado decorated with Chinoiserie mouldings up to hand level, the paper can take over up to the ceiling, augmented, if you like and as 18th-century ladies did, with cut-outs of extra birds. Other Chinese artefacts are at once at home here, from little blue and white tea dishes to great barrel-shaped ceramic garden seats. On the floor, put down a Chinese carpet, in royal blue with colourful flowers and butterflies, or pale camelhair with blue and white flowers.

The muralled bathroom is another way to enjoy a multi-coloured flower theme. Some of the most successful designs are those formal bouquets copied from the overdoors of Italian palazzi or French wainscots. On silver-gray grounds, the faded flowers, all the shades of nature, can turn a bathroom into a Petit Trianon and have the added advantage of growing old gracefully. If either of these schemes are worked, then the rest of the room should be kept plain white with at most a marble surround for the tub or splashback.

Simple country bathrooms can be decked up as chintzy living rooms with rundown sofas strewn with flowery quilts of every colour and size. There will be big mirrors framed in gold or mahogany, coloured prints of flowers and some pretty 19th-century hand-painted china – Rockingham, perhaps, or Chantilly. Some houses make the kitchen the room to congregate. This one uses the bathroom for family conferences, afternoon tea and comfortable chats. It has come a long way from the gloss-painted hospital room of 50 years ago.

Set Details & Fabric Keys

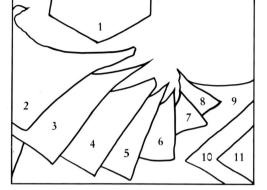

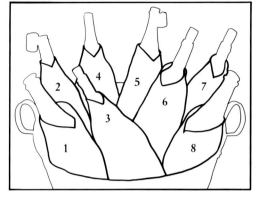

PERIOD WARES, pages 30-1
1   Cup and saucers, The Dining Room Shop
2   Meat plate, Botanical Beauties, The Dining Room Shop
3   Dinner plate and gravy boat, Spode, Blue Colonel, The General Trading Company
4   Tile, Pilkington, Poynter, The General Trading Company
5   Coffee pot, Hutschenruther, Liberty
6   Victorian tea plates, The Dining Room Shop
7   Plate, Putnams
8   Tile, Poppy and Insect, early English Delft, Fired Earth
9   Bowl, Cauloon Blue May, Putnams
10 Meat dish, Asiatic Pheasants, The Dining Room Shop
11a Coffee cup, Mason, Denmark, Liberty
11b Teacup, Spode, Fontaine, The General Trading Company
11c Cup, Gien, Oiseau Bleu, The General Trading Company
12 Coffee pot, Spode, Italian, The General Trading Company
13 Plate, Royal Persian, The Dining Room Shop
14 Jug and plates, Burleigh ware, Scilla, The General Trading Company
15 Bowl, Burleigh, Poynter, Recollections, The Victoria and Albert Museum Shop

PERIOD THEMES page 36
1   Comoglio Aaris, Guy Evans
2   Antique fabric
3   Stansislas, 9935.92, Nobilis-Fontan
4   Honeysuckle, Liberty
5   Lampas Amboise, 8922, 03, Prelle
6   C7025, 13, Turnell & Gigon
7   Verona, 892/59, Romo Fabrics
8   Gothic Hearts, Belinda Coote
9   Infroissable gaugrage velvet, 15121, Marechal Lyantey, Percheron
10 Bellini, Red, Watts
11 Rose Hilliard, Watts

FADED PALETTE page 42
1   Thorny Rose, Regular, Bennison
2   Du Barry, Marius Boudin Collection, Les Olivades
3   Palais Royal, Jason D'Souza Designs
4   Rose Tree, Hodsoll McKenzie
5   Pomegranate, Hodsoll McKenzie
6   Monochrome Roses, Pink, Bennison
7   Bailey Rose Linen, 2001/04, Sand/Pink, Colefax & Fowler
8   Rosevine, faded blue, Bennison

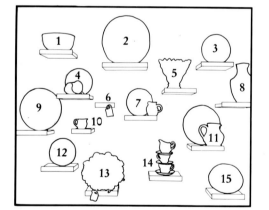

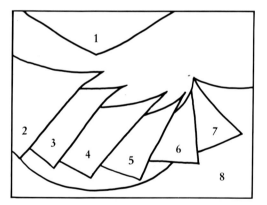

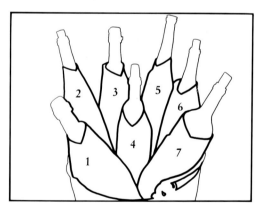

MODERN WARES pages 32-3
1   Bowl, Annie Doherty
2   Dish, papier mâché, Lucy Ogden
3&4 Plates and jug, Mary Rose Young
5   Vase, Belen Ceramics, Liberty
6   Cup, Mary Rose Young
7   Plate and jug, Liz Riley, Liberty
8&9 Vase and platter, Annie Doherty
10   Spongeware jug, Emma Bridgewater, The General Trading Company
11   Plate and jug, Lindy Brockway
12   Jonquil plate, Isobel Dennis
13   Punch bowl, Mary Rose Young
14   Cups, Annie Doherty
15   Bowl, Janice Tchalenko, Dart Pottery

MODERN THEMES pages 41
1   Tapestry Flower, Designers Guild
2   Pretty Roses, Celia Birtwell
3   Mary's Room, 12043/4333, Collier Campbell
4   Leafdance, 12277/708, Collier Campbell
5   Charisse, Hill & Knowles
6   Matin de Juin, 11318, Manuel Canovas
7   Tapisserie, Designers Guild
8   California Positive, Celia Birtwell

BRIGHT PALETTE page 44
1   Delft, 11224, Anthracite 80, Manuel Canovas
2   1949, 03, Souleiado
3   Grosvenor, 9, Titley & Marr
4   Tiverton 2, MP 9201, Monkwell
5   1980, 03, Souleiado
6   Nature, 701/679/8, Alton-Brooke
7   Passiflore, Topaze, Lelievre

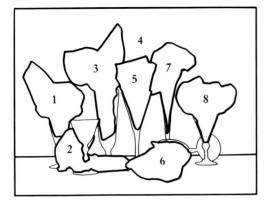

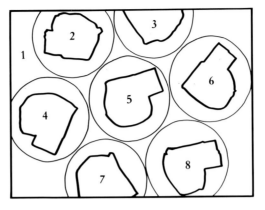

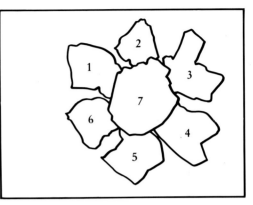

MONOCHROME FLORALS page 48
1 Pali 11146, Azur 55, Manuel Canovas
2 Gonfazoniere, 16, John Stefanidis
3 Pembridge Paisley, Celia Birtwell
4 Floral Positive, Bennison
5 Ulverston, 2, Titley & Marr
6 Wimbledon, TG 5607, Turnell & Gigon
7 Toile de Velay, 7556, 003, Marvic
8 Charlecote, Titley & Marr

SMALL PATTERNS page 52
1 Cornflowers, Sapphire Multi Mustard, Laura Ashley
2 Jalmont, Comaglio 22, Guy Evans
3 Troubadour, Cobalt, TA 0115 119, Les Olivades
4 Spring Parterre, F241A, Osborne & Little
5 1061, 03, Souleiado
6 East Buff, Waverly
7 1745, 01, Souleiado
8 1401, 00, Souleiado

FLOWERS IN BUD page 56
1 Rose sprig, 1157/04 Green, Colefax & Fowler
2 Fuchsia, 1070/01 Red, Colefax & Fowler
3 Victoria, 662/01, Romo Fabrics
4 Little Flowers, Bennison
5 Colin Maillard, 9930.81, Noblis-Fontan
6 Rosebud 5, MP 9111, Monkwell
7 Brook Collection, Colefax & Fowler

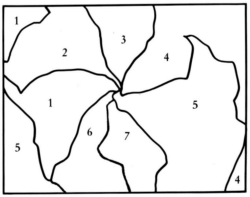

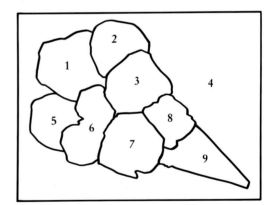

RAINBOW FLORALS page 51
1 Mysore, 11214, Rouge 05, Manuel Canovas
2 Snow Bramble, Osborne & Little
3 Cottage Garden, Liberty
4 Balalaika, 7093.2, Percheron
5 Winchester, Titley & Marr
6 Benita, 11311, Manuel Canovas
7 Le Jardin des Muses, 05, Prelle
8 Out of Africa, 2038/4, Percheron

LARGE PATTERNS page 55
1 Grenada, Manuel Canovas
2 Longport, The Design Archives
3 Brahmane, Manuel Canovas
4 Norwich, French blue/old gold, Stuart Renaissance Textiles
5 Girardon, Sahco Hesslein
6 Devonshire, 2054-1, Lorenzo Rubelli
7 Tulip, Titley & Marr

FLOWERS IN BLOOM page 58
1 Rose Garden, F452-01, Osborne & Little
2 Dublin Bay, 40071, A051 green/pink, The Design Archives
3 Melbourne 90053, A003 green, The Design Archives
4 Florestan, Poppy, Liberty
5 Flowervyne, MP9170, Monkwell
6 Rose Hall, E8508, Ramm Son & Crocker
7 Rose Bouquet, 68322, Cole & Son
8 Bailey Rose, 1051/01 Pink, Colefax & Fowler
9 Victoria, RF 657/06, Romo Fabrics

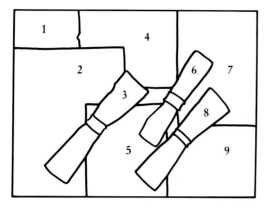

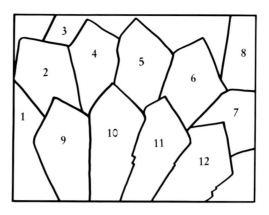

BOTANIC DESIGNS page 63
1 Serendip, 11300, Anthracite 80, Manuel Canovas
2 Bagatelle, Nina Campbell
3 Aldeburgh FR1, A1195-02, G.P. & J. Baker
4 Ferns, A0845-01, G.P. & J. Baker
5 Tulip, Titley & Marr
6 Ridgelyburn, B0712-05, G.P. & J. Baker
7 Botanical, BLF 3970, Rich & Smith
8 Auricula, F240a, Osborne & Little
9 La Hore, 7111-1, Lorenzo Rubelli

INSPIRATION FROM INDIA page 66
1 Seringapatam 9024, Prelle
2 Roman Stripe, Hodsoll McKenzie
3 3018/1759, 01, Souleiado
4 Madura 11217, Safran 27, Manuel Canovas
5 Raj 90080, A012 Red, The Design Archives
6 Palmetto, GP 63656 F, Brick & Indigo, Warner Fabrics
7 Fayence Cavaillon F552/05, Osborne & Little
8 Paisley Kashmir, 851/14, Romo Fabrics
9 Indira 11098, Ecru 92, Manuel Canovas
10 Malabar, Bennison
11 Indore: Sienne, TF 9906:4, Les Olivades
12 Caliph 31600, A020 Sand/Turk, The Design Archives

THE RED ANTHOLOGY pages 72-3
1 Scroll Bouquet, Hodsoll McKensie
2 Carisbrooke, Titley & Marr
3 Beauly Red/Beige, Nina Campbell
4 Bradenham, Red, Nicholas Herbert
5 Amadeus, 70200, Red A012, The Design Archives
6 PR7506-1, Sanderson
7 Indiennes Fou-Sin, Nina Campbell
8 Borders Pieta, QQ0126.141, Les Olivades
9 MF5054, Claret 7, Monkwell

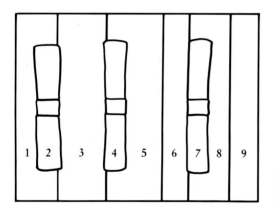

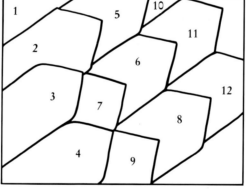

DIAGRAMMATIC DESIGNS page 64
1 Pomone, 4312, 27 Ajonc, Manuel Canovas
2 Kew Collection, Trefoil, Hill & Knowles
3 Mistletoe stripe, Blue, Bennison
4 Morocco, Bennison
5 Tourette, 4309, Paille/Marine 27, Manuel Canovas
6 Arno, Stuart Renaissance Textiles
7 Tulipan, Marvic
8 Embarras Militaire, TA 0060, Les Olivades
9 Magritte, 12744, Sahco Hesslein

INSPIRATION FROM CHINA page 68
1 Les Magots, 11294, Indienne 01, Manuel Canovas
2 Fusuma, RF 437/01, Romo Fabrics
3 Mandarin, 11157, Rouge 06, Manuel Canovas
4 Belen, 11040, Bleu Blanc 60, Manuel Canovas
5 Bienaimée, 11216/42, Manuel Canovas
6 Patience, Putnams
7 China Collection, F224B, Osborne & Little
8 Le Dernier Empereur, Manuel Canovas
9 Pavillon de Bidaine, 11286, Manuel Canovas
10 China Collection, F220A, Peony Pots, Osborne & Little
11 Chinese Silk, Crimson Multi Ivory, Laura Ashley
12 China Collection, F222A, Osborne & Little

THE YELLOW ANTHOLOGY pages 94-5
1 Les Fleurs de Lys, Gold/Green/Off-White,
   Warner Fabrics
2 Edwardian Roses, Warner Fabrics
3 Melrose - Brook Collection III, Colefax & Fowler
4 1619, 14, Souleiado
5 Percier Damask, Rich Gold/Stone, Warner Fabrics
6 PR7457-3, Sanderson
7 Bernini, 044A635, green/yellow, Hodsoll McKenzie
8 Verity, Putnams

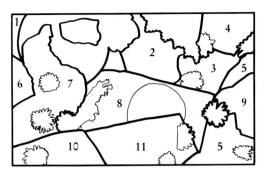

THE BLUE ANTHOLOGY pages 110-11
1   Brahmane, 11287, 50, Manuel Canovas
2   Rhapsody, Sanderson
3   Vivian, 11313, Bleu 55, Manuel Canovas
4   PR7434-3, Sanderson
5   1507, 19, Souleiado
6   PR7553-3, Sanderson
7   London Damask 1101, The Design Archives
8   Harriet, Putnams
9   Bramble Leaf, 054A, Slate, Hodsoll McKensie

THE WHITE ANTHOLOGY pages 146-7
1   Ribbons & Bows Lace, Laura Ashley
2   Bagatelle, Artois Stripe, Nina Campbell
3   Antique linen & lace cloths
4   Dogrose 777530, Cole & Son
5   Portobello Paisley, Celia Birtwell
6   Harting, 2-Ecru, Titley & Marr
7   Baskets & Bows Lace, Laura Ashley
8   California Positive, Celia Birtwell
9   Boudin Riban Vert, Tr 9919:V, Les Olivades
10 Sackville Imtr, 747727, Cole & Son
11 Paradise, White 97, Manuel Canovas

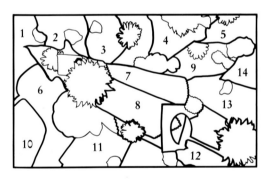

THE GREEN ANTHOLOGY pages 128-9
1   Shepherdsbush, T45602, Turnell & Gigon
2   Acanthus, Cole & Son
3   Bracken, FR5, R1244/0, G.P. & J. Baker
4   Rectory Wall, FR5 S1152-02, G.P. & J. Baker
5   Willow, Liberty
6   Norwich, Stuart Renaissance Textiles
7   Hortense 4, MP 9187, Monkwell
8   Bourcy, Sanderson
9   Documenta II, Corylus, F453-01, Osborne & Little
10 Documenta II - Bantry, F457-01, Osborne & Little

THE MULTICOLOURED ANTHOLOGY pages 164-5
1   Newnham Country, Sanderson
2   Rose & Fern, Cream/Pink, Jean Monro
3   Auboron, 817/46, Natural, Romo Fabrics
4   Rose & Peony, Sanderson
5   Grapes all over, G.P. & J. Baker
6   Country Bouquet, 30040, A002 Blue, The Design Archives
7   Viikuna - Marimekko Collection, MF3688-117, Rich & Smith
8   Chang show - Valentino, VL4001205, Rich & Smith
9   Briarwood, 484/01, Romo Fabrics
10 Victorian Ribbons, 1, Titley & Marr
11 Marlborough, PR 7572/1, Sanderson
12 Ratamo - Marimekko, MF3683-123, Rich & Smith
13 Coucareu, Les Olivades
14 Louis Philippe, 60078, A073 Beige, The Design Archives

PROPS

MONOCHROME FLORALS, page 48: *glasses* (right to left): small from The Dining Room Shop; small with wine from The Dining Room Shop; tall bowl from The General Trading Company; flared from Habitat; tall flared, engraved with a band of flowers, from Habitat; glass on side from The General Trading Company.

RAINBOW FLORALS, page 51: *glasses* (right to left): green/blue "Murano" from The Conran Shop; green from The Dining Room Shop; deep blue handmade Spanish from Habitat; orange "Murano" from The Conran Shop; green from The Dining Room Shop; bubbly blue from Habitat; wide green from Habitat; very tall pale pink from The Conran Shop; engraved red with grapes and leaves from The Dining Room Shop.

BOTANIC DESIGNS, page 63: selection of *antique napkin rings* from The Dining Room Shop.

DIAGRAMMATIC DESIGNS, page 64: selection of *antique napkin rings* from The General Trading Company.

THE RED ANTHOLOGY, pages 72-3: *fabric-covered chest* from Putnams; *pin cushion* from Tobias and the Angel; *cup* from The Dining Room Shop; *Burleigh flower plate* from Putnams; *"Antieke Polychrome Flower" tile* from Fired Earth; *roses* from Paula Pryke.

THE YELLOW ANTHOLOGY, pages 94-5: *Brazilian Delft flower tile* from Fired Earth; *"Waechtersbach" coffee cup* from Heals; *"Union" sprig jug* from Putnams; *brown and yellow plates* from The Dining Room Shop; *appliqué mat* from Tobias and the Angel; *flowers* from Paula Pryke.

THE BLUE ANTHOLOGY, pages 110-11: *hand-painted eggs* from Liberty; *"Fontaine" Spode cup* from The General Trading Company; *tiles*: top right English Delft "Petunia and Insect" by Fired Earth; half hidden "Poynter" by Pilkington from The General Trading Company; *"Scilla" saucer* by Burleigh from The General Trading Company; *antique "Asiatic Pheasants" plate* from The Dining Room Shop; *flowers* from Paula Pryke.

THE GREEN ANTHOLOGY, pages 128-9: *cream and green Italian plate* from Divertimenti; small *"Evasion" plate* by Gien from Liberty; *needlepoint bag* from Tobias and the Angel; *tile* from Fired Earth; *banana leaves* from Paula Pryke.

THE WHITE ANTHOLOGY, pages 146-7: bottom *plate* from Barratts; top *bone china "Oceanside" plate* by Wedgwood; *19th-century child's plate with flowers* from Tobias and the Angel; *flowers* from Paula Pryke.

THE MULTICOLOURED ANTHOLOGY, pages 164-5: *flowered "Summertime" dish* by Royal Winton from Putnams; *hand-painted Indian picture frame* from Liberty; *flour/sugar shaker* by Royal Tudorware from Putnams; *needlepoint pin cushion* from Tobias and the Angel; *cup* by Mary Rose Young; *embroidered tablecloth* from Tobias and the Angel.

The Directory

Afia Carpets
60 Baker Street
London W1M 1DJ
England
Rugs and carpets.

Alton-Brooke
5 Sleaford Street
London SW8 5AB
England
AMERICAN SUPPLIER:
BERGAMO FABRICS
INC
979 Third Avenue
New York NY 10022
Fabrics.

Laura Ashley
150 Bath Road
Maidenhead
Berks
SL6 4YS
England
AMERICAN SUPPLIER:
BILL HAYES
1300 MacArthur Boulevard
Mahwah
New Jersey 07430
*Fabrics, wallpaper,
furniture, china and
accessories.*

G.P. & J. Baker
PO Box 30
West End Road
High Wycombe
Bucks HP11 2QD
England
AMERICAN SUPPLIERS:
LEE JOFA
800 Central Boulevard
Carlftadt
New Jersey 07072
BAILEY & GRIFFIN
1406 East Mermaid Lane
Philadelphia PA 19118
BRUNSCHWIG & FILS
979 Third Avenue
New York NY 10022
Fabrics and wallpapers.

Bennison
16 Holbein Place
London SW1W 8NL
England
IN AMERICA:
BENNISON
73 Spring Street
New York NY 10012
Fabrics.

Celia Birtwell
71 Westbourne Park Road
London W2 5QH
England
AMERICAN SUPPLIER:
CHRISTOPHER
HYLAND
Suite 1714,
979 Third Avenue
New York NY 10022
Fabrics.

Bridgewater Ceramics
739 Fulham Road
London SW6 5UL
England
Spongeware pottery.

Lindy Brockway
5 Daisy Lane
London SW6 3DD
England
Potter.

Burger
39 rue des Petits
Champs
75001 Paris
France
BRITISH SUPPLIER:
PERCHERON
97-9 Cleveland Street
London
W1P 5PN
AMERICAN SUPPLIER:
LEE JOFA
800 Central Boulevard
Carlftadt
New Jersey 07072
Fabrics.

Nina Campbell
9 Walton Street
London
SW3 2JD
England
AMERICAN SUPPLIER:
OSBORNE & LITTLE
979 Third Avenue
New York NY 10022
*Fabrics, interior design
service.*

Manuel Canovas
7 place Furstemberg
75006 Paris
France
IN BRITAIN:
CANOVAS
2 North Terrace
Brompton Road
London SW3 2BA
IN AMERICA:
CANOVAS
979 Third Avenue
New York NY 10022
MANUEL CANOVAS
P.D.C. 8687 Melrose
Avenue
West Hollywood
C.A. 90060
Fabrics.

Jane Churchill
137 Sloane Street
London
SW1X 9BZ
England
AMERICAN SUPPLIER:
COWTAN & TOUT
979 Third Avenue
New York NY 10022
*Fabrics, interior design
service.*

Cole & Son
18 Mortimer Street
London W1A 4BU
England
AMERICAN SUPPLIER:
CLARENCE HOUSE
211 East 58th Street
New York NY 10022
Fabrics and wallpapers.

Colefax & Fowler
39 Brook Street
London W1Y 2JE
England
AMERICAN SUPPLIER:
COWTAN & TOUT
979 Third Avenue
New York NY 10022
*Fabrics and wallpapers.
Interior design service.*

Collier Campbell
63 Old Town
London SW4 0JQ
England
AMERICAN SUPPLIER:
P. KAUFMANN INC
51 Madison Avenue
New York NY 10010
Fabrics and furniture.

The Conran Shop
Michelin House
81 Fulham Road
London SW3 6RD
England
*Fabrics, furniture and
accessories.*

Belinda Coote
29 Holland Street
London W8 4NA
England
*French tapestries, tapestry
fabrics and painted
furniture.*

Dart Pottery
Shinners Bridge
Dartington
Totnes
Devon
TQ9 6JE
England
Ceramics.

Isobel Dennis
c/o Clockwork Studios
38 Southwall Road
London SE5 9PG
England
*Ceramics: one-off pieces in a
wide range of designs.*

The Design Archives
79 Walton Street
London SW3 2HP
England
AMERICAN SUPPLIERS:
COWAN & TOUT
979 Third Avenue
New York NY 10022

BAKER FURNITURE
2219 Chose Drive
High Point
North Carolina
NC 27263
CLARENCE HOUSE
211 East 58th Street
New York NY 10022
RANDOLPH & HEIN
1 Arkansas Street
San Francisco
California 94107
*Fabrics, including woven silk
brocades, classic stripes,
chintzes and toiles de Jouy.*

Designers Guild
271 and 277 King's Road
London
SW3 5EN
England
AMERICAN SUPPLIER:
OSBORNE & LITTLE
979 Third Avenue
New York NY 10022
Fabrics and wallpapers.

The Dining Room Shop
62-4 White Hart Lane
London SW13 0PZ
England
*Furniture and accessories for
the dining room.*

Divertimenti
139 Fulham Road
London SW3 6SD
England
Kitchenware and ceramics.

Annie Doherty
167 Highbury Hill
London N5 1TB
England
Potter.

Dorma
PO Box 7
Lees Street, Swinton
Manchester
M27 2DD
England
*Fabrics, wallpapers and
bedlinen.*

Jason D'Souza Designs
38 Graham Street
London N1 8JX
England
*Fabrics based on 17th- and
18th-century designs.*

Etamine
2 rue Furstemberg
75006 Paris
France
BRITISH SUPPLIER:
DESIGNERS GUILD
271 and 277 King's Road
London SW3 5EN
England
Fabrics.

Guy Evans
51a Cleveland Street
London W1P 5PQ
England
AMERICAN SUPPLIER:
CLASSIC REVIVALS INC.
1 Design Center Place
Suite 545 Boston
Massachusetts 02210
Fabrics and wallpapers.

Fired Earth
102 Portland Road
London W1 4LX
England
Decorative tiles.

**The General Trading
Company**
144 Sloane Street
London SW1X 9BL
England
*Rugs, soft furnishings and
accessories.*

Thomas Goode & Co
19 South Audley Street
London W1Y 5DN
England
China and accessories.

Linda Gumb
9 Camden Passage
London N1 8EA
England
Antique textiles.

Habitat
196 Tottenham Court Road
London W1P 9LD
England
*Furniture, rugs, fabrics,
wallpapers, accessories, glass,
china, dried flowers.*

Heals
196 Tottenham Court Road
London W1P 9LD
England
*Furniture, china, rugs, dried
flowers, baskets, bedlinen
and accessories.*

Nicholas Herbert
83 Lower Sloane Street
London SW1 W8DA
England
AMERICAN SUPPLIER:
CLARENCE HOUSE
211 East 58th Street
New York NY 10022
Fabrics.

Hill & Knowles
133 Kew Road
Richmond
Surrey TW9 2PN
England
AMERICAN SUPPLIERS:
CLARENCE HOUSE
211 East 58th Street
New York NY 10022

CLASSIC REVIVALS
6th Floor, Suite 545
1 Design Center Place
Boston
Massachusetts 02210
*Fabrics, wallpapers,
furniture and stencils.*

Hinchcliffe and Barber
Studio 5
Town Farm Workshop
Dean Lane
Sixpenny Handley
Salisbury, Wiltshire
England
*Pottery and resist hand-
blocked fabrics.*

Hodsoll McKensie
52 Pimlico Road
London SW1W 8PL
England
AMERICAN SUPPLIER:
CLARENCE HOUSE
211 East 58th Street
New York NY 10022
Fabrics.

Indigo Seas
123 North Robertson
Boulevard
Los Angeles CA 90048
USA
*Old and new furniture,
fabrics and accessories.
Interior design service.*

Isis Ceramics
23 Western Road
Oxford
OX1 4LF
England
*Pottery designs taken from
17th- and 18th-century
Delftware.*

Ralph Lauren
980 Madison Avenue
New York NY 10021
USA
IN BRITAIN:
RALPH LAUREN
144 New Bond Street
London W1Y 9FD
England
*Wallpapers, fabrics,
furniture, home furnishings
and fragrances.*

Lelievre
13 rue du Mail
75002 Paris
France
IN BRITAIN:
LELIEVRE
16 Berners Street
London W1P 3DD
AMERICAN SUPPLIER:
ANDRE BON
979 Third Avenue
New York NY 10022
Fabrics.

Liberty
Regent Street
London W1R 6AH
England
IN AMERICA:
LIBERTY
Rockefeller Center
5th Avenue
New York NY10020
Fabrics, wallpapers, furniture and accessories, rugs and accessories.

McKinney Kidston
1 Wandon Road
London SW6 2JF
England
Period curtains or drapes and poles.

Marvic Textiles
12-14 Mortimer Street
London W1N 7DR
England
AMERICAN SUPPLIER:
BRUNSCHWIG & FILS
979 Third Avenue
New York NY 10022
Fabrics.

Monkwell
10-12 Wharfdale Road
Bournemouth
Dorset BH4 9BT
England
Fabrics and wallpapers.

Jean Monro
53 Moreton Street
London SW1V 2NY
England
Fabrics.

Neal Street East
5 Neal Street
London WC2H 9PU
England
Furniture, fabrics and accessories from the East.

Nobilis-Fontan
29 rue Bonaparte
75006 Paris
France
IN BRITAIN:
NOBILIS-FONTAN
1-2 Cedar Studios
45 Glebe Place
London SW3 5JE
IN AMERICA:
NOBILIS-FONTAN
1823 Springfield Avenue
New Providence
NJ 07974
Fabrics.

Lucy Ogden
1a Walpole Terrace
Kempton, Brighton
East Sussex
England
Papier mâché ware.

Les Olivades
Avenue Barberin
13150 St Etienne-du-Gres
France
IN BRITAIN:
LES OLIVADES
16 Filmer Road
London SW6 7BW
Fabrics from Provence.

Osborne & Little
304-8 King's Road
London SW3 5UH
England
IN AMERICA:
OSBORNE & LITTLE
979 Third Avenue
New York NY 10022
Fabrics and wallpapers.

Raymond O'Shea Gallery
89 Lower Sloane Street
London SW1W 8DA
England
Flower prints.

Pallu & Lake
Unit M27, Chelsea Harbour
Lots Road
London SW10 0XE
England
Fabrics.

Pepe Penalver
Valdegovia
28034 Madrid
Spain
BRITISH SUPPLIER:
BRIAN YATES
3 Riverside Park
Caton Road
Lancaster LA1 3PE
AND 4 Berners Street
London W1P 3AG
Fabrics.

H.A. Percheron
97-9 Cleveland Street
London W1P 5PN
England
Fabrics and trimmings.

Prelle
5 place des Victoires
75001 Paris
France
BRITISH SUPPLIER:
GUY EVANS
51a Cleveland Street
London W1P 5PQ
AMERICAN SUPPLIER:
CLASSIC REVIVALS
Suite 545
1 Design Center Place
Boston, Mass. 02210
Fabrics.

Paula Pryke Flowers
20 Penton Street
London N1 9PS
England
Florist.

Putnams
55 Regent's Park Road
London NW1 8XD
England
Fabrics and antiques.

Ramm, Son & Crocker
13-14 Treadaway Technical Centre, Treadaway Hill
Loudwater,
High Wycombe HP10 9PE
England
AMERICAN SUPPLIER:
BRUNSCHWIG & FILS
979 Third Avenue
New York NY 10022
Fabrics and wallpapers.

Rich & Smith Interior Collections Limited
North Street,
Stoke-sub-Hamdon,
Somerset TA14 6QR
England
Fabrics and wallpapers.

Romo Fabrics
Lowmoor Road
Kirkby-in-Ashfield
Notts NG17 7DE
England
AMERICAN SUPPLIER:
TOWN & COUNTRY LINEN CORP.
295 5th Avenue
New York NY 10016
Fabrics and wallpapers.

Lorenzo Rubelli
Palazzo Corner Spinelli
San Marco 3877
30124 Venice
Italy
BRITISH SUPPLIER:
PERCHERON
97-9 Cleveland Street
London W1P 5PN
AMERICAN SUPPLIER:
BRETEUIL
221 East 48th Street
New York NY 10019
Fabrics.

Sahco Hesslein
Kreuzburger Str.19
D-8500 Nurnberg 51
Germany
IN BRITAIN:
SAHCO HESSLEIN
101 Cleveland Street
London W1P 5PN
AMERICAN SUPPLIER:
IAN WALL
979 Third Avenue
16th Floor
New York NY 10022
Fabrics.

Arthur Sanderson
53 Berners Street
London W1P 3AD
England

IN AMERICA:
ARTHUR SANDERSON
Suite 403
979 Third Avenue
NY 10022
Fabrics, wallpapers, linen.

B.C. Sanitan Ltd
Unit 12, Nimrod Way
Elgar Road
Reading
Berkshire RG2 OEB
England
Period-style flower decorated sanitaryware.

Shyam Ahuja
32 Dr A.B. Road
Worli
Bombay 400018
India
BRITISH SUPPLIER:
ALTON-BROOKE
5 Sleaford Street
London SW8 5AB
IN AMERICA:
SHYAM AHUJA
201 East 56th Street
Third Avenue
New York NY 10022
Fabrics and accessories.

Souleiado
39 rue Proudhon
B.P. 21
13151 Tarascon Cedex
France
IN BRITAIN:
SOULEIADO
171 Fulham Road
London SW3 6JW
AMERICAN SUPPLIER:
PIERRE DEUX
870 Madison Avenue
New York 10014
Traditional cotton fabrics.

John Stefanidis
261 Fulham Road
London SW3 6HY
England
Fabrics, furniture and objects. Interior design service.

Stuart Interiors
Barrington Court
Barrington, Ilminster
Somerset TA19 ONQ
England
AMERICAN SUPPLIER:
CLASSIC REVIVALS
6th Floor, Suite 545
1 Design Center Place
Boston
Massachusetts 02210
Designers and weavers of early English and European fabrics, including worsted damasks, brocatelles, lampas and double cloths. Interior design service.

Titley & Marr
141 Station Road, Liss,
Hampshire
GU33 7AJ
England
AMERICAN SUPPLIER:
CLARENCE HOUSE
211 East 58th Street
New York 10022
Fabrics.

Tobias and the Angel
68 White Hart Lane
London SW13 0PZ
England
Antique dealer.

Today Interiors
122 Fulham Road
London SW3 6HU
England
AMERICAN SUPPLIER:
PAYNE
3500 Kettering Boulevard
PO Box 983 Dayton
Ohio 45401
Fabrics.

Turnell & Gigon
Unit M20
Chelsea Garden Market
Chelsea Harbour
Lots Road
London SW10 OXE
England
Fabrics.

Kenneth Turner Flowers
19 South Audley Street
London W1Y 6BN
England
Florist.

Un Jardin . . . En Plus
82 rue de Montigny
95100 Argenteuil
France
IN BRITAIN:
100 Mount Street
London W1Y 5JF
IN AMERICA:
20224 South Normandie Avenue
Torrance CA 90502
Fabrics, hand-painted furniture, curtains, china and glassware.

The Victoria and Albert Museum Shop
Cromwell Road
London SW7 2RL
England
Reproductions of period china and accessories.

Vigo Carpet Gallery
6a Vigo Street
London W1X 1AH
England
Antique and modern rugs and carpets.

Warner Fabrics plc
Bradbourne Drive
Tilbrook
Milton Keynes
MK7 8BE
England
AMERICAN SUPPLIER:
GREEFF
150 Midland Avenue
Port Chester NY 10573
Fabrics and wallpapers.

Watts & Co
7 Tufton Street
London SW1P 3QE
England
AMERICAN SUPPLIER:
CHRISTOPHER HYLAND
Suite 1714
979 Third Avenue
New York NY 10022
Woven fabrics and hand-printed wallpapers.

Waverly
79 Madison Avenue
New York, NY 10016
USA
Fabrics.

Mary Rose Young
Oak House
Arthur's Folly
Parkend, Lydney
Gloucestershire GL15 4JQ
England
Potter.

Josiah Wedgwood & Sons
Barlaston, Stoke-on-Trent
ST12 9ES, England
AND 158 Regent Street
London W1R 5TA
IN AMERICA:
WATERFORD & WEDGWOOD
41 Madison Avenue
New York NY 10010
Fine bone china in a wide range of designs.

Mary Wondrausch
The Pottery
Brickfields
Compton, nr. Guildford
Surrey GU3 1HZ
England
Slipware pottery - traditional pots, commemorative pieces.

Zoffany
63 South Audley Street
London W1Y 5BF
England
AMERICAN SUPPLIER:
CHRISTOPHER HYLAND
Suite 1714
979 Third Avenue
New York NY 10022
Fabrics and wallpapers.

Index

Acknowledgments

The author and publishers would like to thank the following house-owners and museums:
Rosie and Michael Addison, The American Museum in Bath, André de Cacqueray Antiquities, Charleston Farmhouse, Jane Churchill, Comoglio showroom in Paris, château de Compiègne, château de Courance, Hannerle Dehn, Vera and Murray Gordon, Linda Gumb, Jenny Hall, Lyn von Kirsting, Patou von Kirsting and Richard Irving, Judith and Martin Miller, Morris-Jumel Mansion, Tom Parr, Dick Schneidler, Second House Museum, Dennis Severs, Skansen Open Air Museum in Stockholm, Keith Skeel, Jenny Shin, Jacqui Small, Ken Turner, Lillian Williams, Mary Wondrausch and Mary Rose Young.

PHOTOGRAPHY CREDITS
Key: b bottom; c centre; l left; r right; t top.

All location photographs by James Merrell for Mitchell Beazley except for: 15 Bill Batten; 20bl/bc/br Vigo Carpet Gallery; 43 Bill Batten; 45 Sanderson; 50 Dorma; 57 Dorma; 59 Dorma; 62 Osborne & Little/Nina Campbell; 67 Designers Guild; 92tr B.C. Sanitan Ltd; 99 Designers Guild; 107br Warner Fabrics plc; 112 Ralph Lauren; 118 Ralph Lauren; 126 Laura Ashley; 136 Sanderson; 162tl Osborne & Little/Nina Campbell.

All studio photography by Lark Leigh Gilmer for Mitchell Beazley: 31, 32, 36, 41, 42, 44, 48, 51, 52, 55, 56, 58, 63, 64, 66, 68, 72-3, 94-5, 110-11, 128-9, 146-7, 164-5.

All illustrations kindly lent by Raymond O'Shea of the O'Shea Gallery, 89 Lower Sloane Street, London SW1W 8DA.